365 JOURNAL WRITING ideas

A YEAR OF DAILY JOURNAL WRITING PROMPTS,
QUESTIONS **&** ACTIONS TO FILL YOUR JOURNAL
WITH MEMORIES, SELF-REFLECTION,
CREATIVITY **&** DIRECTION.

ROSSI FOX

ISBN-13 978-0-9576793-0-6
ISBN-10 0957679300

With thanks to Kiran for diligently proofreading the hardcopy edition.

Published By Rossi Fox.

This book is dedicated to my family for putting up with such a daydreamer and to you my fellow or soon to be, never too far away from a pen and notebook, journal writer.

CONTENTS

Introduction	xi
How to use this book	2
The Tips & Tricks	
Journal size & style	6
Commit to your choice	7
Why make the time?	7
Journal O'Clock	8
The fear of the blank page	10
Give your journal an identity	12
Titling, dating & tagging	13
You this read wrong	13
For your eyes only	14
Get messy	15
Lost & found	16
Flashbacks	16
Picture perfect	17
Gratitude journal	18
Inspirational tokens & mementos	20
Year-long photography challenge	22
Basic prompts	24
Hello There Blank Page	26
The Prompts	30
The Weekly Actions	150
The Photography Prompts	176
Hello	230

The Quotes

Adventure	180
Age	181
Anger	182
Beauty	183
Change	184
Cheerful	185
Courage	186
Creativity	188
Death	190
Education	191
Family	192
Friendship	193
Goals	194
Gratitude	198
Happiness	202
Health	204
Inspirational	205
Kindness	208
Life Lessons	208
Love	212
Mistakes	213
Money	214
Motivational	215
Nature	218
Positive Thinking	220
Science	221
Success	221
Worry	224
Writing	226

ISN'T IT MYSTERIOUS
TO BEGIN A NEW JOURNAL...
I CAN RUN MY FINGERS
THROUGH THE FRESH CLEAN PAGES
BUT I CANNOT GUESS
WHAT THE WRITING ON
THEM WILL BE

MAUD HART LOVELACE

Introduction

Hello and welcome to 365 Journal Writing Ideas, my name is Rossi and it is very nice to meet you. Before we begin, do any of the following ring true for you?

- Do you have a desire to create a record of your life, to fill a journal or diary with memories, your inner most feelings, ideas, creativity and ambitions?

- Is there a collection of blank journals building up on your bookshelf that you have not touched since buying them because you are scared of ruining them? Instead they sit and wait on your bookshelf unfulfilled like the last Christmas tree left in the store.

- Does it feel like the intimidating blank journal page is saying, "Really? You think you are good enough to write on me do you?"

- Have you started a journal before but stopped after only a few entries because you found it repetitive and boring writing about what you had for breakfast, again? Or did you find it too intense, demanding and time consuming?

- Perhaps you are a writer or blogger who wants to knock the wind out of writers block next time it shows up?

If so, you are in the right place as I wrote this book for you.

So before we start why not make yourself your favorite drink and put on your comfortable clothes, you know the ones you would dare not wear outside of the house. Let's unlock the potential of your journal and enjoy the next 365 days of you-time...

HOW TO USE THIS BOOK

Just to let you know in advance the journal prompts & actions in this book are not dated so you can start from prompt No.1 & weekly action No.1 at any point in the year.

You will need:
- A journal or notebook.
- A pen, which does not bleed through the page.
- A camera or camera phone.
- A glue stick or tape.
- A few envelopes slightly smaller in size than the pages of your journal.
- Optional: Paints, colored pencils & pens.
- Courage to take on 'the blank page'.

Journaling Tips & Tricks

Here you will find a collection of ideas and hacks to help you get the most out of your journal writing practice. Learn how to beat the blank page to start your journal writing practice, how to make the time to write, how to organize your journal/diary, ideas on how to add some visual interest, a collection of alternative journal prompts, a photography challenge checklist, and more.

365 Journal Writing Prompts & Questions

A yearlong guided self-exploration through daily writing prompts. To help you use your journal/diary as a place to remember where you have been (memoir), appreciate where you are now (gratitude) and decide on where you going (goals).

Not only helping you gain clarity, closure and purpose but also resulting in your very own mini memoir or life journal keepsake.

Mixed in amongst the reflective journal writing questions are creative writing prompts, light hearted questions and short story writing idea generator tables to help get your creative writing juices flowing allowing you to have some fun with your journal.

For the short story idea generator tables use a dice to select at random 1 of 6 plot ideas from each of the 3 columns. Then combine them to create the plot line for your short story. If you do not have a dice handy, simply write down 3 numbers each from 1-6 at random without looking at the table of plot ideas first.

For example 3 6 5 you would use the 3rd prompt from column A, the 6th prompt from column B and the 5th prompt from column C.

You can use the 365 prompts in sequence completing one a day (more if you wish) to build a full and diverse journal in just 10-20 minutes a day, or as an occasional resource to help you beat writer's block.

52 Weekly Actions

Along with your trusty journal, complete one action each week over the 365 days to make the next 52 weeks of your life just that little bit more interesting.

At the beginning of each week, check the weekly actions to receive your weekly prompt/mission to be completed over the 7 days.

As part of the weekly actions you will be asked to occasionally complete a photography prompt. Keep your camera or camera phone with you and keep an eye out for any opportunities to take as many interesting photos of the subject as you can.

Interpretation of the prompt word is totally up to you. Then report back to your journal with your favourite 1-3 photographs. You can use the photography prompt list as a source of photography subject ideas at anytime.

Quotes

I have collected and ordered by subject over 400 quotes and proverbs to be used as an extra source of inspiration, wisdom and starting points for your journal writing practice. I am a self-confessed quote addict. You too?

Note to the digital journal writers: All of the prompts and actions in this book are applicable to those using a journaling app on a computer, smart phone or tablet.

Just keep in mind whenever you are prompted to glue something in to your journal simply take a photograph of it and add to the journal entry. Remember to back up often.

The Tips & Tricks

Journal Size & Style

This is a completely personal choice, as your journal will need to be a place you are happy to write in, carry and be seen in public with.

Ask yourself do you prefer a blank page or do you need lines to keep your words from looking like they have been on a night out? Can the paper handle the type of pen you want to use without bleeding through? Do you prefer a journal to be stitched together like a book or spiral bound?

Do you want your journal to have an image on the cover or do you want it plain? Are you planning on customizing the cover with images you want? Do you want a ribbon to mark your current page? An elastic strap to keep it shut?

Spend some time at a bookstore or stationers and get a feel for as many journals and notebooks as you want. Having worked in a stationary store before, I know it is around the notebooks where people spend the most time (there and the glittery gel pens). Picking one journal up, putting it back, picking it back up, then back down, picking up another and so on.

So do not worry about the staff wondering if you are acting suspiciously, they will be used to it.

The most popular journal size we sold was around A5 paper size (148mm x 210mm). I too personally prefer the A5 as they are easier to carry around, they are less intimidating to get started with and look more like the journals from the movies once complete.

I have experimented with a lot of different journals over the years and my personal favorite is the Large Moleskine Ruled Notebook because it is lined, has a back pocket and an elastic strap.

If the journal you have chosen does not have a pocket in the back, glue in an envelope of a slightly smaller size to your journal on the inside of the back cover. This way you can collect 'bits and pieces' as you go to be added to your journal pages at a later time.

Commit To Your Choice.

Whichever you choose or if you decide to use one you have already bought. Commit to it. This is now the journal you are going to use for the next 365 journal writing days. You will probably go through more than one over the next year so you can experiment with another style for your next one if you wish.

Just do not stop and start again in another journal because you are not 'feeling it'. This is it.

Why Make The Time?

Making the time to journal can be difficult, jobs need doing, children need feeding, dogs need walking. Writing in the evening can be a great way to clear the mind but can be interrupted by unplanned nights out, temptation to watch a great TV show or the day could of been so long, the last thing you want to do write when all you want to do is crash out.

So I make the effort to journal first thing in the morning. Well it used to be an effort at first, as I used to hate mornings (really hated mornings) but now I feel like I have cheated myself of something if I don't do it.

Like with exercise it is too easy to dismiss it as something 'I don't have time for' or 'I'm too tired'. So I like to think of journal writing like mining for precious stones. Sometimes it is going be easy then at times it will feel difficult and you will face thoughts and emotions you would rather keep buried, but by digging deep and clearing the dirt and clutter you will find your diamonds.

Your shiniest diamonds are going to be moments of clarity, acceptance, closure, creativity, ideas, direction and purpose.

They are why we should make the time.

Journal O'Clock

If you to want to journal first thing but find it difficult to wake up when you are still not done with yesterday, this is a technique I created through many trial and errors to make myself more of a morning person.

Use two alarms, one set for the time you actually want to get up at, then the other for 30 minutes before the first. The first alarm to go off will be by your bed and you can turn it off for a guilt free 30-minute lie in. The second alarm to go off will be by your bedroom door, now you are up. Stay up. Even though your bed will be calling you back. Go into the kitchen and make yourself a drink to wake yourself up with. Now for the best part, get back into bed with your journal. The next 45 minutes are yours and yours alone to journal in bed.

Open this book and your journal and go with it. It will get your mind going for the day and I have found for myself the benefit of journaling first thing is that although we are slower physically in the morning (lots of yawning, stubbing toes on the corner of the wall etc) our minds are pretty sharp as the events of the day have not cluttered them up yet. There is probably a scientific study somewhere backing this up.

Once you have finished your daily journal writing you could spend the rest of your Journal O'clock time flicking through your journal, writing out your list of to-dos for the day or reading a chapter of a book.

Example of my routine:
  6:00   Alarm by bed for 30 minute lie in.
  6:30   Alarm by bedroom door, get up and make coffee.
  6:35   Get back into bed for journal writing and reading.
  7:15   Get on with the rest of my day.

Now how much better does this sound compared to starting your day by throwing your alarm clock off of the wall because you are convinced the people in charge of time have got things horribly wrong and you should still have another 4 hours of sleep due. Rushing around the house while still getting ready, eating breakfast while putting on your shoes and telling yourself the daily lie of "I'm going to wake up earlier tomorrow".

Give the Journal O'clock routine at least 7 days to see if it works for you. Of course journaling at night is a great way to get things off your mind and prepare for a restful nights sleep. Try both and see which works, you yourself will know which is best for you.

Keeping your journal by your bed can also be useful for 2 more reasons:

1   For a restless or worry filled night. Open your journal and just get what is on your mind out onto the paper, better to let your journal deal with it than have it going around your head all night long.

2   For moments of night-time genius. How many times have you thought of an amazing idea at night but instead of turning on the light and getting up to make a note you've told yourself "I'll remember it in the morning". Only to wake up remembering you had an idea, but you have no clue what it was.

The Fear Of The Blank Page

This is the biggest hurdle many people face when wanting to begin journal writing. You have made the time but now you have this beautiful piece of craftsmanship sitting in front of you. In your mind you are picturing a fascinating journal filled with thoughts, dreams, images and memories. Yet the fear of 'ruining it' prevents you from even starting.

If this is a problem for you, do not worry because I have included an introduction prompt to help you conquer the first blank page.

I too was so intimidated by the blank page in my first journal you would have been forgiven for thinking it had snapping jaws or shouted insults at me every time I opened it. After many months of hesitation, I realized my need for perfection was literally getting me nowhere. So I now repeat the following mantra to myself whenever I need to stop my perfectionist in its tracks:

A DONE SOMETHING IS BETTER THAN A PERFECT NOTHING.

It is based on the saying 'done is better than perfect', which for some reason I couldn't quite buy into, perhaps because part of me believes perfect is better than done. So by adding 'something is better than nothing', I can believe in that completely.

I write this on the page I feel intimidated by to break the ice and let it know who is in charge. After all, it is a piece of paper.

It is also useful to use in day-to-day life, for example when procrastinating about something you really need to get done, such as filling out a form, making an important phone call, etc.

So if at any point over the next 365 days should you feel intimidated by your perfectionist (disguised as the fear of the blank page) write the mantra down into your journal.

Remember you cannot ruin an empty journal by writing in it. It would be like saying you ruined an empty swimming pool by filling it with water. It is not something rare and precious, after all there could be another million copies of the exact same blank journal in the world.

A journal was never meant to be empty, it was created to help you, so let it.

Scribble/doodle/write into the box below. Why? Because if you can do it in a 'real book', writing in a journal will be a breeze.

Give Your Journal An Identity

A good way to push yourself past the fear of the blank page is to read the prompts in this book as though they are questions being asked of you by a journalist or TV talk show presenter. It turns your journal writing into more of a conversation and also prevents you from using brief one-word answers; after all you wouldn't give Oprah Winfrey a one-word answer would you? It also helps you write more because it feels like someone is actually listening to your words.

Give your journal a name to address it by or you could pretend you are writing to a friend, a family member, a historical figure, a fictional character, a celebrity or business personality you admire or even to your higher-self or higher being of your choice. Anyone or anything that helps you open up. You could even address your answers to me if it helps, you can read the about me on page 230 to put a face to the questions.

Another way to ensure you gain the most possible benefit from your practice is to aim to fill an entire page in your journal per prompt. This will prevent you giving short answers and increase the likelihood of the prompt sparking an idea or memory. It also creates a more interesting keepsake and remember you are digging for diamonds.

HELLO THERE GOOD LOOKING
I AM YOUR JOURNAL & MY NAME IS

NICE TO MEET YOU! LET'S GET JOURNALING...

TITLING, DATING & TAGGING

At the top of every entry write down the prompt question or just the prompt question number so you can refer back over them. On the outside top corner of each page note the date and on the bottom outside corner tag the journal entry with a #hash-tag. For example if the entry is about your parents you could add #Family #Mom #Dad etc. This makes flicking back over your journal easier, rather than having to scan over every page you can just look at the bottom of each page to see what it was you wrote about.

Once you have finished a journal (great feeling) be sure to label the spine with a date. For example if you wrote in the journal from the 1st of February 2013 to the 20th of September 2013 you would write 01/02/13 - 20/09/13. It just helps for future reference and you can build up a nice ordered collection on your bookshelf (is that my borderline OCD talking again?).

YOU THIS READ WRONG

Do not worry about your spelling, grammar or punctuation being perfect. Your journal writing is not going to be assessed. Just let loose and let the words run free without the fear of the grammar police pulling you over and ruining your flow.

 Photocopy or cut out & stick into the front of your journal

For Your Eyes Only

Even with an amazing hiding space for your journal (if you feel like hiding it), the fear of people finding your journal and reading something about you or them they might not like is enough to make you drop your pen and bin your journal right now. So whichever journal size you decided on, measure one page and note the dimensions somewhere in the back for future reference.

With this information browse through some magazines, catalogues, newspapers and cut out images and pages that catch your eye. Cut them to size and take 5, fold them half and keep them in the back pocket or envelope in your journal. These can be used to cover over any pages where you have vented about someone or written something you would rather no one else ever read. Scribble over your words and simply glue the magazine page/image over the journal page.

So you will feel better for getting things off of your chest, you do not need to worry about anyone seeing it and you have a nice image in your journal.

AnothertechniqueIoccasionallyuseistowritewithnospacesitcanfeelq uitestrangewritinglikethisatfirstbutquiteoffputtingforanyoverthesh ouldernosyreaders.

Get Messy

Use your journal as a space to get creative, messy and experimental. Some suggestions are:

- Prepare pages with a bit of paint for some colour before writing on them.
- Paint on pages just for the sake of it; enjoy spreading the paint around the page.
- Create collages; images you are drawn to, things you want or collections of images of the same color etc.
- Fill a page with colorful sweet wrappers.
- Fill a page with rubber stamp prints.
- Cover a page with an image pulled from a magazine and use it as a background for a journal entry and write on top of it.
- Finger painting.
- Become an impromptu fashion designer and sketch out some ideas or collect images of styles you like.
- Spread paint around a page using an old gift card then using the edge of the gift card write into the paint to reveal the page beneath. Page size quotes look great like this.

Have fun. It adds texture to your journal and gives it a 'crunch' when closing it. Note: I personally find acrylic or poster paints work better than watercolors, as watercolor paints can soak through most standard journal paper types.

Lost & Found

 Hopefully this will never be needed but just in case, on the inside cover of your journal stick in a small envelope with a $10 note inside with a small note saying:

"Please use this money to post my journal back to me at (name and a work address). It would mean the world to me and please keep any change for yourself. Thank you for your act of kindness."

Seal the envelope and write on or next to it:

"If you have found my journal please open this envelope".

This may seem unnecessary at the start of your journal-writing journey but once it is filled with memories, ideas and dreams the $10 will seem like nothing compared to having your priceless personal keepsake returned.

Flashbacks

Use your journal to record any fleeting memories. Include as much detail as you can recall. You do not need to remember the specifics like the date or time of the memory, just the details of the moment. Imagine they are like the 'flashbacks' characters in movies and TV shows have to build their back-stories.

Simply start an entry with **I remember when...**

Picture Perfect

When adding photos to a journal entry it can be tempting to add a lot together but you will end up with more of a photo album than a journal. You should be selective (pretend you are an editor of a magazine) and only add one or two to illustrate the entry.

If you can't resist adding more, glue in an envelope onto a page and keep them together that way or make a small collage of images.

Keep a piece of card to scale of a photo size you would like to add to your journal in the back pocket. Then when you know you want to add a photo you can draw the outline and write around it. I use a 4" x 2.5" template because I can fit 8 photos onto an A4 sheet of photo paper. Also drawing around business cards and sticking in Post-It notes can be a good way to make space for a photo you wish to add later.

We tend to leave our photographs trapped inside our digital cameras, phones and computers. So on payday why not buy (or on special occasions ask for) a gift voucher for a photo print shop or for wherever you buy your printer ink and photo paper from.

This way you will always be in a position to release your photos and physically hold, add them to your journal, share and keep them for future generations. Imagine if your parents did not have that amazing box of random family photos. Do you have half as many physical photographs?

Gratitude Journal

Even though a number of the prompts in this book are gratitude based why not boost the feel good benefits of your journal writing practice by writing down 1-3 things you are grateful for after every journal entry.

They can be things you have, have experienced or feel grateful for simply existing so you can one day enjoy them. Some areas to pull from are:

Experiences
Food & Drink
Health & Body
Material Goods & Services
Money & Success
Nature
Passions & Interests
People
Places

Also do not be afraid to repeat gratitude entries. I used to be so hung up on the idea of having to have completely unique entries, until I realized it is all about what you are feeling. If you are feeling grateful for something again, write it down again.

Gratitude is gratitude, simple.

WHATEVER YOU APPRECIATE

AND GIVE THANKS FOR

WILL INCREASE

IN YOUR LIFE

Sanaya Roman

Inspirational Tokens & Mementos

A list of things to keeping adding to your journal:

- Your photographs
- Old family photographs
- Photo-booth strips
- Flyers
- Business cards
- Appointment cards
- Recipes
- Magazine articles
- Postage stamps
- Quotes, Prayers or words of wisdom
- Handwritten letters
- Thank you notes
- Postcards (whenever you are somewhere new, post yourself a postcard)
- Letters or emails of good news
- Advice from books
- Images from magazines, catalogues and brochures that catch your eye
- Drawings
- Doodles
- Seat placement name cards
- Name cards from conventions and networking events
- Images of things you want to own or experience
- Greeting cards
- Funny & amusing images
- Invitations
- Travel tickets
- Hotel key cards
- Concert, movie & theatre tickets
- Maps
- Examples of typography you like
- Receipts from restaurants & bars you enjoyed.

In fact anything flat that you find interesting or inspiring. You do not need to know why you find it so interesting, just keep it. You never know one of these little tokens could be the starting inspiration point for something big. Plus they add some texture and visual impact to your journal.

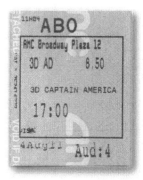

If something catches your eye but is not flat or 'glueable' take a photograph of it to glue in later or maybe draw it.

If something like a magazine or blog article is too big, you can fold it once over, then again and glue one side to the page. It will then open up full size when you want.

Alternatively summarize the key points of the article into your journal. For blog articles note the website URL into your journal, like a really retro (pen & paper) bookmarking tool.

Year-long Photography Challenge Checklist

Your photography mission (should you choose to accept it) is to over the next 12 months see how many of the following you can photograph. Stick the photographs into your journal.

- A sunrise
- A sunset
- Horses
- The ocean
- A forest
- A wild open space
- An ice-cream sundae
- Fireworks
- The view from your bed
- A wise looking tree
- A bird in flight
- A jumping cat
- A sleeping dog
- A self-portrait using a photo-booth
- A celebrity
- A city skyline
- Colorful flowers
- Street art
- A portrait
- A group portrait
- The view from a window in your home
- A busy dance floor
- The flag of your country blowing in the wind
- A castle, palace or state building
- A breathtaking view
- Dancers
- The contents of your bag laid out
- A baby animal

- A large crowd
- A flower or plant in 3 stages of its life; seed, sprout and in full bloom
- A roller-coaster
- A historical landmark
- Moving water
- A kiss
- A home baked cake.
- A market stall
- A portrait of a stranger
- A Christmas tree
- A cocktail
- A swimming pool
- A spider's web first thing in the morning
- Clouds
- Someone you love
- Something you love
- A rainbow
- A snowman
- Rain on the window
- Bokeh
- Something yellow
- Something blue
- Something green
- Something red
- Something pink
- Something orange
- Something black
- Something white
- Something you really want

- ....

Basic Prompts

Here are a few simple but really useful journal prompts to add to the back of your journal as a quick on the go resource:

- How are you feeling?
- What do you need to do?
- What is not sitting well with you?
- If only...
- I am loving...
- Tell me about a few things that happened today/yesterday.

End of week review:
- What did you do?
- What went well this week?
- What did you learn?
- What are your goals and intentions for next week?

These prompts can also be used as an alternative to any of the 365 prompts you do not want to use or feel do not apply to you.

A DONE SOMETHING IS BETTER THAN A PERFECT NOTHING

Hello There Blank Page

The first page, "so white and pure like fresh snow, it would be such a shame to write on it" I hear you say. So we aren't going to, you can stick an inspiring image onto the first page at a later date but right now we are going behind it's back, literally.

Flick to the next page and now let us conquer this double blank page spread by writing out the following to set out your intentions for next year of your life. Write them in a simple list format or randomly around the pages. Either way remember, a done something is better than a perfect nothing.

Over the next 365 days I give myself permission to...

play
rest
love
vent
grow
shine
learn
explore
simplify
color outside of the lines
be loved
be strong
be daring
dream big
be grateful
help others
be creative
laugh more
ask for help
be successful
accept myself
try new things
be determined
create my own life
be kinder to myself
repeat myself if I am not heard
repeat myself if I am not heard
keep an open mind
rise above negativity
let go of past hurts & regrets
celebrate my daily achievements
grab new opportunities with both hands

Congratulations! The blank page has been defeated and you have set the tone for the upcoming year. Ready? Great, now onwards to the next 365 days.

The Prompts

1

What does 'happiness' mean to you? Would you describe yourself as a naturally happy or an unhappy & worried person? Tell me about a time when you felt really happy and about a time when you made someone else feel happy.

✓ 2

Create a list of resolutions you would like to keep over the next 365 days. Write as many as you can. Now circle the 3 that mean the most to you and for each one make a promise to your journal:

I promise to (blank). I want to do this because achieving this would mean (blank). My reward will be (blank).

I promise to (blank). I want to do this because achieving this would mean (blank). My reward will be (blank).

I promise to (blank). I want to do this because achieving this would mean (blank). My reward will be (blank).

I am fully aware that at times I will break my resolutions but instead of throwing in the towel and quitting, I will quickly get back on track without feeling any sense guilt or failure.

Signed ....

Combine one prompt from each column to create a
plot-line for a short story.

	A	B	C
1	On the 11:00 train from London to Paris	a school teacher	discovers a shocking secret.
2	On a cold winters night	an under appreciated personal assistant	performs an act of bravery.
3	In the jungles of South America	a passionate University professor	travels 100 years into the future.
4	In an underwater research facility	a grumpy old man	accidentally travels back to the time of the Dinosaurs.
5	On the canals of Venice	an introverted ballet dancer	fights for survival as the world has been overrun by zombies
6	On a desert island	a chef who hates spoons	must prevent a nuclear disaster.

4

Tell me about one of your earliest memories. Write down anything you can remember.

5

If you had to be someone else for 24 hours, who would you choose and why? What would you do?

6

Would you rather be less attractive and extremely intelligent or extremely attractive and less intelligent? What do you think the pros and cons of each combination would be?

7

List as many things that you can see right now that you are grateful for?

8

What do you need to accept?

9

Tell me about an adventure you would love to have.

10

Write about a dream you can remember. Go into as much detail as possible; fill in the gaps with your imagination. Capturing your dreams in a mind-map can also be good source of inspiration for a later date.

11

Tell me about one of your most memorable experiences with nature.

12

Make a list of all the things you would do or buy if you won the lottery jackpot.

13

What are you waiting for?

14

In no particular order fill a double page spread in your journal with a list of people, things and places that make you happy.

15

What 'excess baggage' are you carrying around? Create a list of all the negative things you would like to drop off at lost property. Such as a regret, a negative self-belief, a grudge or a past event etc. Tell me how releasing them would make you feel?

16

If you could click your fingers and be anywhere else right now, where would you be and why? What would you be doing? What would you see, hear, smell and taste?

17

Write about meeting someone you admire (real or fictional) in an empty elevator, you have 3 minutes to make conversation.

What will you say? What do you want the outcome of the conversation to be? You could even write out the conversation in a script format.

18

At home find a keepsake box or rummage through a 'junk' draw and find something that has a sentimental meaning to you, write about it. What or who does it represent? Alternatively find some old photographs and tell me about one of them.

19

Who would you want to play you in a movie of your life and why? Who could play the other important roles? What songs would you choose for the soundtrack? Create the playlist.

20
What is some of the best advice you have ever received?

21
I am grateful for my sense of sight because...

22
At the top of the page write 'I am awesome because...' or 'I am wonderful because...'

Now write a list dedicated to the awesomeness of you. All of your achievements, successes, talents, skills, quirky interests, qualifications, best experiences & proudest moments. Big and small in no particular order just write them down. Going right back to when you were a child.

23
I would like to improve my relationship with (blank) because...

What are the main problems? What solutions can you think of? What are some of the good points to the relationship? For example at the worst, this relationship may have taught you about how not to treat other people. What would the benefits of this relationship working better be?

24

Pick a song, a favorite or completely at random and use a line of lyrics as a title of a short story. Write about whatever the lyrics bring to mind.

25

Tell me about a 'perfect moment' you have experienced. Where were you, who was there, what happened, how did you feel? How does it feel remembering this moment?

26

Think of 5 different ways you could treat yourself by spending less than $5. Action: Do one of them this week.

27

If all of the karma you have earned in your life so far came back around to you today, do you think it would it be good or bad? Why?

If good, how would you like to be rewarded? If bad, how do you think you could improve it from today onwards?

28

I am grateful for my sense of touch because...

29

What does 'courage' mean to you? When have you been courageous for yourself? When have you been courageous for others?

30

Create a list of all the places in the world you would like to visit. Ignore any money or logistic limitations; just write down your dream list in no particular order.

31

Combine one prompt from each column to create a
plot-line for a short story.

	A	B	C
1	In a secret underground government research facility	a calm and peaceful yoga instructor	saves the life of an enemy.
2	On a golden beach	a firefighter with a fear of heights	finds an old coin which brings good luck.
3	While scuba diving	a member of Royalty	finds a compass and a treasure map.
4	In New York	a vegetarian Lion	falls in love.
5	At the Great Pyramids of Egypt	a socially awkward geek	is offered a dream job.
6	While climbing a mountain	a blind man	receives an important phone call.

32

Tell me about your earliest memories of school. Can you remember your teachers name and appearance? What were they like? What were your friend's names? What things were important to you then? What did you enjoy?

33

What would the name of your autobiography be and why? Title each chapter with a brief description.

34

If you could relive one memory of your life over again, which would you choose and why?

35

I am grateful for my sense of taste because...

36

How are you?

37

Create a list of experiences you want to have enjoyed in your life.

Such as climbed a mountain, attended a party on a yacht, stayed in a 5 star hotel, been an extra in a movie, met your idol, volunteered at a wildlife sanctuary, etc.

Ignore any money or logistic limitations; just write down your dream list in no particular order.

38

Walk around a bookstore or library and open a random book and select a page. Write down the first sentence of the second paragraph. Now write about whatever came to mind when you read the sentence. If you cannot make it to a bookstore or library use a book from your own bookshelf or eBook collection.

39

Tell me about one of the best gifts you have ever received.

40

In your journal write a letter to yourself at 13 years old. What advice would you give?

41

If you could go back in time and change one thing, would you take the opportunity? Why?

42

I am grateful for my sense of smell because...

43

In your journal write a letter (you will never send) to someone you have unresolved issues with. Who you are upset with, feel anger towards or to someone who has left you feeling 'off centre' after something they have said or done.

You can even write the letter to yourself about a regret you are holding onto.

Explain how you are feeling. Get it all out.

If you are ready, at the end of the letter I encourage you to try and write I forgive you, I'm sorry, thank you, I love you. It is not for their benefit but for your own.

This is from the Hawaiian practice of forgiveness known as Ho'oponopono. Created to help release you from holding onto negative emotions about a situation. Therefore allowing you to move forward.

44

Create a list of all the achievements you want to have accomplished in your life.

Such as the ability to speak another language, wrote a book, mastered a martial art, started your own business, raised a happy family, be a talented cupcake baker, earned a degree etc.

Ignore any money or logistic limitations; just write down your dream list in no particular order.

45

Think of a cause you are passionate about, or a disagreement you have had. Now write about it from the other side's perspective.

Why did they or why are they doing what they are doing? What drives them to do what it is you disagree with? From this point of view can you see any areas where both sides could come to a compromise?

46

Tell me about someone you miss. Either someone who has passed away, moved or you simply drifted apart from. What experiences did you share? How did they make you feel? What did you learn from them?

Write a letter in your journal to them updating them on your life since you last saw them.

47

In your journal write a letter to yourself 10 years in the future.

48

What makes you lose track of time?

49

I am grateful for my sense of hearing because...

50

Tell me about something you regret. Then after tell me about what letting go of this regret would do for your wellbeing.

Or tell me about a mistake you have made in your life. Big or small. What happened? Was it really that bad? Beneath it tell me at least 3 good things to come out of the situation. Circumstances, experiences, lessons learned or any new opportunities?

51

Make a list of all the things you want to do, try and experience that you would find scary and challenging at the time, but would feel amazing after having conquered them.

Such as cage dived with a great white shark, bungee jumped, held a tarantula spider or snake, solo dined in a busy restaurant, sang at a karaoke bar, etc.

Ignore any money or logistic limitations; just write down your dream list in no particular order.

52

Look out of the nearest window and write in vivid detail what you can see starting from left to right. Imagine you are telling someone who is not tall enough to look out of the window, use as much detail as possible.

53

Tell me about a time you overcame a difficult situation? What did you learn?

54

What would your superhero power of choice be? What would you do with your amazing super power? What would your super hero or super heroine name be? What would your costume be like?

Or if you wanted to become a super villain what would your name be? What would your abilities and ambitions be? Describe your secret liar where you make all your plans for world domination.

55

Tell me about a time when you made what had once seemed impossible, possible.

56

Looking back on yesterday, do you feel like you have lived that day over & over before? If so, how could you mix things up?

57

What do people say you are good at?

58

Tell me about something you want to do or try but your little nagging & self-doubting voice tells you not to. Making you hesitate to even take the first step.

What reasons does it come up with? Let it have full control for a few moments; write down all the doubts it brings up. Now put a line through or scribble out each of its objections and stick an image representing your desire over their words. On top of the image write about how good proving that little critical voice wrong will feel.

59

Today eavesdrop on a conversation for a few moments. Use what they were talking about as a starting point and continue their story in your journal. Change the names if you know the people.

60

When you were younger what did you want to be when you were older and why?

61

If you found a magic lamp what 3 wishes would you ask the Genie for? What would each mean to you? No wishing for extra wishes, not my rules, the Genie's rules.

62

What cages have your fears built around you? How could you open the door?

63

Write a letter or an email to a company praising a member of their staff who recently helped you. Draft it out in your journal first. Report back to journal.

64

What do you worry about the most?

Are your worries realistic or do they always play out far worse in your head than in reality?

"When I look back on all these worries, I remember the story of the old man who said on his deathbed that he had had a lot of trouble in his life, most of which had never happened."
- Winston Churchill

65

What would you do if you knew you could not fail?

66

Combine one prompt from each column to create a
plot-line for a short story.

	A	B	C
1	In the early hours of the morning	an eccentric fashion designer	is keeping their true identity a secret.
2	In London	a loud & passionate artist	becomes a Genie.
3	At the Eiffel Tower in Paris	a shy student	becomes a giant.
4	At a campsite	a Princess	becomes tiny.
5	In the woods	a playboy Prince	cannot tell a lie.
6	In Rome	a misunderstood Witch	can only tell lies.

67

What were your favorite childhood games? Real or imaginary. What were the rules? Who did you play it with?

68

What would you do if you were invisible for 24 hours?

69

Set a timer for 5 minutes, now for the full 5 minutes do not stop writing. Whatever thoughts cross your mind write them down, do not censor yourself or worry about spelling and punctuation. Just clear all of the mental clutter out onto the page. After the 5 minutes relax and reward yourself.

70

What are some of your favorite feel good songs? Do any of them have special meanings to you? Create a play list.

71

What would you change about yourself or your life if you could? Why?

72

Write out your own ideal obituary for when you are really old and have peacefully past away in your sleep. Who do you want to be dearly missed by? What do you want to be remembered for? What do you want your list of achievements to have been?

Imagine you could oversee your funeral, what would you want to over hear people saying about you?

Note: This exercise can bring up ambitions and a sense of purpose you were not aware of before. So take hold of it and use to create starting points for your life right now and make a list of the things you would need to do in order to earn this amazing send off and remembrance.

73
What do you appreciate about your life right now?

74
Tell me about your first date. Where did you go, what were they like? Or tell me about how you want your first date to go.

75
In your journal create a double page collage of people you admire. Search for images online or cut them out of magazines. Next to each person write down one word to describe them.

76
Tell me about some of the most important lessons you have learned from your parents.

77
Write a letter in your journal (you don't have to send) thanking someone who gave you great advice or a nudge in the right direction. Tell them how you used their advice.

BE SO GOOD

THEY CAN'T IGNORE

YOU

STEVE MARTIN

78

Excluding people and pets what 3 things would you rescue from a fire? Why is each so important to you?

79

Who would your ideal partner be? What qualities do you want in them? What would you offer them? What will you enjoy experiencing together?

If you are in a relationship, what are your partners best qualities? What do you offer them? What would you like to experience together?

80

Think of your 3 favorite actors; now create a brief movie plot for them together. Give each actor's character a brief history, 3 distinct personality traits, a personal style and a powerful goal.

81

Tell me about a pet you had growing up or a friend's pet. What were they? What was their name? What were they like? Energetic, lazy, loving, scary? Stick in a photo if you have one.

82

How would you spend $1,000,000 in fun and creative ways if it was handed to you right now? No saving it, paying off debts or donating it. You must spend-spend-spend!

83
Who do you love? How do you show them? Do you show them often enough?

84
Create a list of some of your favorite animals, places and events in nature.

85
When do you feel most alive?

86
In detail tell me what your perfect day from start to end would be like?

87
Rewrite a movie ending.

88

Tell me about your time at High School. What are some of your best memories? Who did you spend most of your time with? What were they like? What did you have in common?

What fashion trends and popular crazes swept through your school while you were there? If you had to be defined by one subject in school during your high school years which subject would it of been? What did you want to be when you left high school?

89

Think of 10 different ways you could treat yourself with less than $10. Action: Do one of them this week.

90

If you could do one thing everyday for the rest of your life, what would you choose and why?

91

I am grateful for my family because...

92

Tell me about one assumption that people make about you that is just not true. Why do you think they assume this? How does it make you feel?

93

Describe in detail a walkthrough of your dream home. Do not forget any outside spaces. How would you decorate it? Any stand out pieces of furniture? Even include a rough sketch of the floor plan.

94

Who are some of your favorite fictional characters and why?

95

Tell me about a time when you felt completely free and in the flow of life. Where were you? What were you doing? Who was there? How did you feel?

Write out your star sign and description. Does your personality match your star sign description? What other star signs do you feel describe you? Make up your own, choose 5 of the personality traits you like the most and invent a name and symbol.

Aries (March 21 - April 19)
The Ram
Direct, competitive, impulsive, independent, resourceful, temperamental, trusting, creative, honest.

Taurus (April 20 - May 20)
The Bull
Patient, reliable, practical, determined, stable, observing, artistic/ creative, loyal, stubborn, money focused.

Gemini (May 21 – June 20)
The Twins
Curious, charming, versatile, expressive, persuasive, easily bored, changeable, intelligent, sociable, nervous.

Cancer (June 21 – July 22)
The Crab
Emotional, reactive, intuitive, sensitive, tenacious, caring, sympathetic, moody, traditional, supportive.

Leo (July 23 – August 22)
The Lion
Risk taker, idealistic, ambitious, graceful, proud, dramatic, giving, romantic, dominating, strong.

Virgo (August 23 – September 22)
The Virgin
Efficient, gentle, focused, reliable, methodical, softly-spoken, compassionate, sincere, easily worried, calming, fussy.

Libra (September 23 - October 22)
The Scales
Sociable, careful, creative, convincing, fair, idealistic, indecisive, fickle, laid back, friendly.

Scorpio (October 23 – November 21)
The Scorpion
Intense, passionate, creative, private, intelligent, resourceful, loyal, focused, temperamental, jealous.

Sagittarius (November 22 - December 21)
The Archer
Generous, witty, honest, daring, friendly, confident, optimistic, argumentative, blunt, fun loving.

Capricorn (December 22 – January 19)
The Goat
Responsible, cautious, focused, suspicious, reserved, conventional, reliable, hardworking, unforgiving, successful.

Aquarius (January 20 - February 18)
The Water Bearer
Impulsive, independent, friendly, strong-minded, curious, aware, forward thinker, temperamental, inventive.

Pisces (February 19 - March 20)
The Fish
Imaginative, sensitive, caring, mysterious, adaptable, intuitive, idealistic, spiritual, gullible, trusting.

97
How much money do you think is enough to live comfortably happy on per month? Why?

98
I am grateful for my body because...

99
What inspires you?

100
What skills do you want to learn and why?

Combine one prompt from each column to create a
plot-line for a short story.

		A	B	C
1		On a sunny afternoon	a happy zookeeper	has to fly a plane.
2		In a Doctor's office	a bored football player	is involved in a high speed chase.
3		At a hospital	a terminally ill person	is involved in a shoot out.
4		During a snow blizzard	a billionaire	needs to escape.
5		While watching The Northern lights	a short giraffe	cannot tell a lie.
6		On Christmas Eve	a spy on their first assignment	is kidnapped by mistake.

102

Tell me about a time when you took a big leap of faith or change of direction in your life. What motivated it?

103

What is on your mind?

104

List some of the compliments you can remember receiving, big and small.

105

What do you like about the area where you live?

106

Tell me about one of your fears. Where does it come from? What happens to you physically and emotionally when you are feeling the fear? How does this fear hold you back?

How could you challenge it? Write about how your life would improve after overcoming the fear.

107

What other language(s) would you like to learn and why? Now go and find out how to say the following in one of the languages:

"Hello my name is (blank). I am (blank) years old. I live in (blank) with (blank) and I enjoy (blank), (blank) and (blank). Some of my favorite foods are (blank)."

Now introduce yourself to your journal in your new language. Action: This week take one step towards learning your language of choice.

108

Write a day in the life of someone you know, what do you think they get up to?

109

Tell me about your first job. What did you do? How much were you paid? Who did you work with? What were they like? Did you have to wear a uniform?

If you haven't had a job yet write a list of 'first jobs' you would like and why?

110

In detail tell me about what your perfect meal would be like.

- Starter
- Main course
- Dessert
- Afters
- Drinks

Where would you be?

111

What things in life do you think should be free and available to everyone?

112

List as many things as you can think of in your favorite color.

113

What did you learn from a recent challenge?

Make a list of all the things you want to do but are not making the time for, feel intimidated by or you are simply not feeling motivated enough. These include personal projects, business ideas, catching up with friends and family, vacations etc. Now instead of seeing them as overwhelming and daunting, break them down into 30-day mini goals, then down again into more manageable actions. For example:

My goal is to (main goal) so over the next 30 days I am going to (mini goal) because   (the reason it is important to you). I will start by:

1. Manageable action No. 1.
2. Manageable action No. 2.
3. Manageable action No. 3.

The benefits of doing this will be (list the benefits).

For example if your goal is to write a book:

My goal is to write a book so over the next 30 days I am going to complete one chapter of my book because I have always wanted to write a book and have been putting it off for far too long. I will start by:

1. Scheduling 30 minutes everyday to write.
2. Writing one page per day.
3. Keep my journal with me at all times to record any inspirations and ideas.

The benefits of doing this will be having one chapter complete, I would have developed a habit of writing and the knowledge that if I carry on with writing a page a day by this time next year my book will be complete. Also in my journal I will have a resource of inspiration for future books.

115

Create a fake biography for a stranger you can see or have seen recently. Where did they grow up, what jobs have they had, what have been their happiest and saddest times, what are their secrets and what are their dreams?

116

Tell me about your childhood or current home; take me on a tour in vivid detail. Even add a rough sketch of the layout.

117

In your journal write a list of 10 famous people from the past, present or fictional that you would invite to a dinner party. Why did you choose each one?

Layout the seating plan. What would you serve? What drinks would you offer? Who do you think would get on really well together? Who might need to be kept apart?

118

Tell me about something(s) you can do now that you were not able to do this time last year.

119

Write a list of people you are grateful for being or having had been in your life. Choose one and tell me about why you are grateful for them in more detail.

120
Who or what can always improve your mood?

121
My ideal friends would be...

122
Write the plot for an episode of one of your favorite TV Shows. Don't forget to end on a cliffhanger.

123
Tell me about a graduation or a time when you received an achievement/award. How was the ceremony? Who attended? What did you receive? What did you wear? How did you feel? Add a cringe worthy photo.

124
Find a feel good story from the media; write about how it makes you feel.

125
How would you live your life differently if you knew nobody would judge or disapprove?

126

What do you think about the statement 'crying is a sign of weakness'?

127

How do you express your creativity?

128

My perfect job would be...

129

Find a photo from the news and without reading the article create your own story.

130

Stick in an old family photograph and tell me as much about it as you can. Who are the people? What are they doing? Where was the photo taken?

131

Dedicate a double page spread to some of your favorite quotes.

132

If you could give one piece of advice or a self-belief to every child, what would it be and why?

133

Tell me 5 good things about today or yesterday.

134

Who do you find inspiring? Why?

Job interview skills are always useful to have prepared and ready should your dream job come up. So for each of the following questions, write a simple easy to remember response. Keep them positive and never criticize anyone else.

Pretend your journal is the interviewer.

- Tell us a little about yourself.

- How would co-workers describe you?

- Are you a good team player? Example.

- Give me an example when you went above and beyond the call of duty.

- An example of a time when a suggestion you made was used.

- What are your hobbies and interests outside of work?

- What are some of your weaknesses?

- Where do you see yourself in 5 years?

- An example where you corrected a mistake you made.

- An example where you have dealt with a difficult co-worker or boss.

- Describe yourself in 5 words.

- If you had to be any animal what would you be and why?

Combine one prompt from each column to create a
plot-line for a short story.

	A	B	C
1	On Christmas Day	an accident prone nurse	discovers they have won the lottery.
2	On New Years day	a vampire who gets light headed at the sight of blood	meets someone who looks identical to them.
3	At a birthday party	a ghost who is scared of other ghosts	shares a kiss with a stranger.
4	At an anniversary party	a mischievous mermaid	falls in love with someone their friends and family would disapprove of.
5	After drinking too much wine	a jolly writer	discovers they are the only one left on the planet.
6	While wishing for a better life	an attractive assassin	discovers they can read minds.

137
Tell me about a time when you really impressed yourself.

138
Draw a line down the centre of a page (or fold and unfold a page in half). Then fill both columns starting with the left side by playing word association with yourself. Start from one of the following words:

Hot
Sharp
Snow
Tree
Secret
Money
Shoes
Words
New
Wonderful
Shady

139

What is your number one goal or intention for the next six months?

Mind map a few ideas and then for the goal that resonates with you the strongest write it out in the present tense, as if you have already achieved it. Starting with I HAVE NOW... or I NOW HAVE...

For example:
- I have now published a book.
- I have now enjoyed a gondola ride in Venice, Italy.
- I now have the latest iPhone.
- I now have enough money for the house deposit.

Then copy your goal/intention on to a piece of paper or Post-It note and keep it somewhere you will see often to help keep you motivated and inspired.

140

What are some of your favorite books and why?

141

What are you proud of yourself for?

142

Use your journal to draft up an 'elevator pitch' for yourself. This is a short introduction to be used when meeting new people should they ask the dreaded questions "so what do you do?" or "tell me a little about yourself".

Include what you do for a living, a current project you are working on or how you spend your days and some interests. Having an elevator pitch ready can take the sting out of the fear of meeting new people in forced situations such as networking *shudders*. Also imagine this is the brief description a talk show host or award host would use to introduce you to the stage. Draft out a few variations of your pitch until you are comfortable with it.

I know from experience the worst question anyone can ask you when you are out of work is "so what do you do?" It can feel like a kick in the teeth, so if you are out of work adapt your pitch to saying what type of job you are looking for or say you have a few ideas in the pipeline then move onto your interests. Remember you are more than what you do for a living; it is your interests that make you interesting.

Note: As an interest travel is useful because it is the easiest conversation starter, it is like throwing a small talk lifeline to the other person for something to talk about. Almost everybody has an interest in traveling. Even if you feel like you haven't been anywhere yet, talking about where you want to go or about where they have been is a great way to break the ice.

143

Fill an entire page writing about something you use daily, without using the name or explaining exactly what it does.

144

Tell me about a memorable moment as a child.

145

If I had an unlimited supply of money I would...

146

Tell me about how an extra £1000 a month would change or improve your life?

147

Some things I love and enjoy about my life are...

148

Tell me how you would react if someone spoke to you as harshly as you criticize yourself. Would you tolerate it, feel hurt or fight back? Why do you let yourself get away with being so hard? How could you be kinder to yourself?

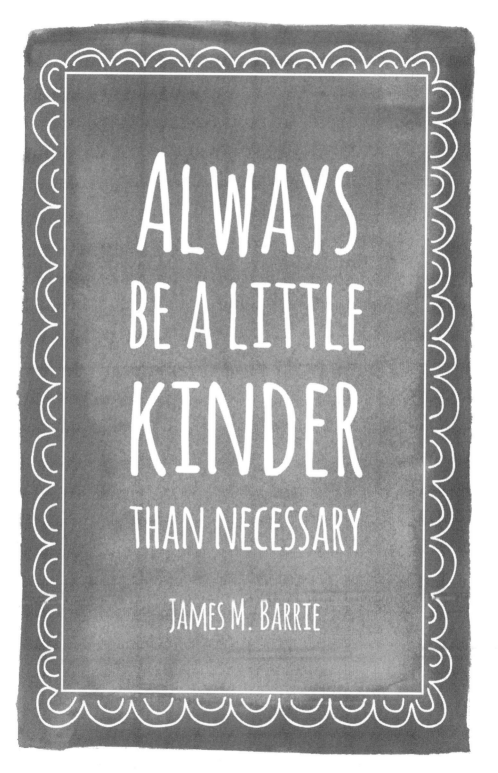

149
Write a list of the books on your 'to-read' list?

150
Write a day in the life of your pet or a friend's pet.

151
Make a list of some of the acts of kindness you have received. Big and small.

152
Create a list of things you would put into Room 101 (banish from the world if your could). From the serious to the small irritating things.

153
Tell me about something you can do or have that other people want.

154
I am truly grateful for my home because...

155
What does the expression 'too live not simply exist' mean to you?

156
Dream life walkthrough.

Fill out the following statement in vivid detail while visualizing your ideal life. Ignore any money or logistic limitations. Just enjoy using your imagination bringing your first class life to life on the pages of your journal.

Hello my name is (blank). I live in (blank), in a wonderful apartment/house with incredible views of (blank) I share my home with (blank). My home is filled with (blank). People who visit describe my home as (blank).

The reasons I jump out of bed in the morning with a spring in my step are (blank). I am thankful to spend my time (blank). One of my proudest moments was (blank).

When traveling I have had the most amazing experiences in (blank), especially the time I (blank). I still can't believe I was brave enough to (blank).

I maintain my wonderful health by (blank). I am grateful for my loving relationships with (blank). I am fortunate enough to have an abundance of money in my life and I am now in a position to contribute to causes and organizations such as (blank).

"Dreams are illustrations... from the book your
soul is writing about you."
Marsha Norman

157
Write a day in the life of a child you know.

158
In as much detail as you can tell me about a memorable family occasion such as a wedding, anniversary, birthday party etc. Add a photo if possible.

159
What would you do if you woke up to discover you were last person on earth?

160
When you are 100 years old, what do you think will have really mattered the most to you?

161
What relationships are you grateful for and why?

162
What do you need to make time for?

163

Write down 3-5 things that you would love to happen to you or accomplish over the next 30 days. Add as much detail as possible and write them in the past tense as if they have already happened. Leave some space in your journal and bookmark the page so in 30 days time you can report back.

Did any of them come true? Are there any signs of them starting to happen?

In 30 days time I will remind you on prompt No. 193.

164

Write a day in the life of one of your favorite wild animals. Where do they live? What other creatures do they interact with? What are their daily challenges?

165

Tell me about your first crush.

166

What would you do if you knew you would not get into trouble for doing anything you wanted for 24 hours?

167

What do you think stands in-between you and your happiness?

168

Tell me about one of your favorite places. Why do you like it?

169

Describe your relationships with your closet family members.

170

If money was no concern, what job would you do for free and why?

Combine one prompt from each column to create a
plot-line for a short story.

	A	B	C
1	After an argument	an ambitious politician	discovers they can talk to animals.
2	On a dance floor in Ibiza	a brave policeman	is given a 2nd chance.
3	While still half asleep	a determined soldier	finds a long lost love.
4	After drinking a magic potion	a passionate redhead	goes against their family to save others.
5	After finding a sealed briefcase	a gentle Gorilla	helps a person make their dream come true.
6	After opening a forgotten jewelry box	a miserable Children's TV show presenter	finds a baby.

172

What was your favorite childhood toy? Describe it in detail. What did it do? What memories does it bring back? What adventures did you share?

173

Who is your famous dream date and why? Where would you go? What would you do? If you are in a relationship who is your famous 'free pass' date?

174

Tell me about one of the most spontaneous and impulsive things you have ever done.

175

What opportunities do you have that you are grateful for?

176

Describe your relationships with your friends.

177

How would you like to make the world a better place?

178

Find 2 random words from a dictionary; together they will be your 'theme'. Write a short story about one of the first images the combination of words brought to mind.

179

Draw your family tree. It does not have to be detailed, just simple lines and names. Go as far back as you know.

180

Which fairytale or Disney movie character are you most similar too and why? Or which would you like to be more like and why?

181

Tell me about one of the best decisions you have ever made.

182

I am grateful for the money I have today because...

183
Which would you choose & why?

Financial security for the rest of your life & living a luxurious lifestyle with every material possession you could ever wish for BUT to be in a loveless relationship.

Or

To be madly in love with someone BUT never knowing where the next $1 was coming from, living in debt and on the edge from month to month.

184
Tell me about some ways you could help others.

185
How would you describe in detail your favorite food or drink to someone who has never tried it before?

186
Who has been a great role model for you? Why? How have they influenced you? Note: You do not have to know them

187
If you could travel back in time, how far back would you go and why? What would you want to see or do there?

188

Through it all, who has been there for you? Write a letter in your journal thanking them.

189

What are you taking for granted?

190

Tell me about what death means to you. Simply the end, reincarnation or is there an afterlife? What scares you about death? Is it leaving people behind? Not accomplishing what you wanted or simply not knowing what is next?

Write about what you are expecting from your afterlife or write about who or what you would like to be reincarnated as the next time around. Use as much detail as possible.

191

Create a list of people you would love to meet. For your top 5 write about why you would like to meet them.

192

Write a review for a movie, book, album or restaurant you recently watched, read, heard or visited.

193

Tell me about one of your biggest adventures so far.

Reminder: 30-day update for prompt No. 163

194

If you could travel into the future, how far forward would you choose to go and what would you hope or expect to see there?

195

Who do you often compare yourself to & why?

196

List your favorite movies.

197

What do you believe in?

No Dreamer is ever too small, No Dream is ever too big

Unknown

198
I wish I had (blank) because...

199
If an Alien asked you to sum up life on earth on only 2 pages of your journal for them to take back to their planet, what would you write?

200
Tell me about your most inappropriate crush.

201
If you had to become a mythical creature like a vampire, werewolf, witch, fairy, mermaid etc which would you choose and why?

202
If someone handed you an envelope containing the exact date and time of your death, would you open it? Why or why not?

203
List your favorite foods.

204
What do you value?

205
I wish I knew (blank) because...

Combine one prompt from each column to create a
plot-line for a short story.

	A	B	C
1	While gambling in a casino	a farmer with a fear of open spaces	discovers a friendly alien.
2	After staying up all night playing video games	a stressed bride	loses their voice before an important event.
3	After falling off a boat	a temperamental international pop-star	does something completely out of character.
4	Whilst feeling sad	a lonely movie star	meets a ghost.
5	Whilst feeling angry	a bickering married couple	finds a talking cat.
6	While feeling happy	a madly in love married couple	becomes best friends with a Panda.

207
Tell me about a time when you have felt lost.

208
List the pros and cons of becoming immortal.

209
If you had to move to another country, what things would you miss the most about where you live now?

210
Tell me about a time when you won something. Hold on to the feeling for a few moments as if it's happening again to you right now. You are a winner! How does it make you feel?

211
Tell me about some of the lessons the school of life has taught you so far. Add a brief summary of the situations that taught you the life lessons.

"Experience is the best teacher."
Unknown

212

Tell me about some of your popular forms of procrastination or your most common excuses for not doing something you know you should.

213

Think about a recent mundane journey; now give it a Hollywood action movie makeover.

Write about it as an adventure: car chases, helicopters, explosions, create exciting characters for those you travel with. Is your bus driver an ex hit-man? Is the passenger in the car next to yours an undercover government agent? Is someone on your train secretly transporting alien technology in their bag?

214

Tell me about one of the bravest things you have ever done.

215

Fill an entire double page spread with your favorite words. Write them in different sizes, different colors and different styles. Keep adding words to these pages when you think of or hear a word you like, fill in any white space with words.

216

Set a timer for 10 minutes, now for the full 10 minutes do not stop writing. Whatever thoughts cross your mind write them down, do not censor yourself or worry about spelling and punctuation. Just clear all of the mental clutter out onto the paper. After the 10 minutes relax and reward yourself.

217

List your favorite material objects (you do not have to actually own them yet).

218

Tell me about a time when any of your negative personality traits such as stubbornness, hesitation or lack of patience have actually helped you.

219
Style vision pages.

Spend some time collecting images that represent how you would like to present yourself to the world through your personal style. Find them online or cut from magazines. Fill a double page spread (or more) in your journal with your 'style sheet'.

Having a style sheet can make shopping and spotting hidden treasures easier as they almost jump out at you because you have an idea of what you are looking for.

220
Create a double page mood board in your journal for your favorite magazine or blog as if you are pitching an idea for an article. Is it a review, interview, story, how-to, report, preview or a photo shoot? Add some example images and a brief summary of your article.

221
Tell me about your first kiss. Who was it with? Where were you? Or how do you want your first kiss to go and with who (change their name if you want)?

222
Is there anything you wish you spent more time doing 5/10 years ago?

223

How do you spend most of your money? How would you like to spend it?

224

Tell me about 5 good things that happened yesterday.

225

What makes you laugh?

226

Home vision pages.

Create a double page (or more) mood board in your journal for your dream home or how you would like to decorate your current home. Include key pieces of furniture, color schemes and inspirational spaces, etc. Find images online or cut from magazines.

227

Think about something you find really beautiful and breathtaking, now in detail describe it in the most mundane, uninteresting and logical way.

228

Tell me about one of the kindest things you have ever done.

229

Create a list of your 'not so useful' talents. Such as losing keys, usually being late, best at making a mess, knowing all the words to a cheesy movie etc.

230

What is something most people do not know about you? Is it because they do not ask or because you keep it a secret?

231

Tell me about how someone has recently helped you? It could be directly or through a service they created/provided.

232

What makes you cry?

233
Travel vision pages.

Fill a double page spread (or more) in your journal with pictures of places you want to visit. Find images online or cut out of magazines. Free travel brochures are a good source of images. Fill the pages with the sights you want to see, places you want to relax, etc.

234
Think about something really mundane and uninteresting to you, now describe in a way that makes it sound breathtakingly beautiful or fascinating.

235
Tell me about one of the greatest moments of your life so far.

236
If you could ask an all knowing higher being of your choice only one question and they had to answer it, what would you ask them? What do you hope the answer would be?

237
If you had to do your life over again, is there anything you would change?

238

Tell me about your favorite holiday/celebration. What do like about it?

239

What are some expectations and demands that you have for yourself? Are they fair or realistic?

240

Health & Body vision pages.

Fill a double page spread (or more) in your journal of images and words that will help motivate you with your health and fitness goals. Include foods you would like to eat more of and any activities you want to do to improve your fitness. Avoid including any unrealistic body inspirations.

EVERYTHING YOU CAN IMAGINE IS REAL

PABLO PICASSO

Combine one prompt from each column to create a
plot-line for a short story.

	A	B	C
1	While attending a wedding	an accountant with dreams of becoming a movie star	learns how to breathe underwater.
2	In a cave	a sarcastic taxi driver	discovers they can fly.
3	In a Russian palace	a werewolf with fleas	must trust no one unless they know the password 'Horizon'.
4	In Sweden	a kind florist	is desperate to fit in.
5	On a hot and dry savannah in Africa	a fire dancer	learns they have more to offer by being themselves.
6	After entering an elevator that is actually a time machine.	a drummer	must work with an enemy to survive.

242

Tell me about your first love. Who were they? What did you love about them? How did you feel when you were together? Or tell me what you are expecting from your first love.

243

Write down 3 things you would like to say to or ask your boss, teacher or someone with authority over you. If you knew you would not get into trouble for it. How would you want them to respond to each?

244

What do you need to avoid or remove in order to improve your life? How do they affect you? How would your life improve if you removed them? How could you make it happen?

245

I am fortunate because...

246

Tell me about the benefits of accepting yourself completely. All of your good and not so good bits.

247

What would you like to explore and learn more about?

248

Pick up a fictional book or open an eBook you have never read, open to page 5, write the first sentence of the 2nd paragraph down and now continue the story to fill the rest of your journal page.

249

Tell me about a time when you were afraid. What happened? How did it make you stronger and what did you learn?

250

My guilty pleasures are...

251

What do you think you would regret not doing, experiencing, being or having when looking back at the end of your life?

252

Tell me about a vacation or a day out you enjoyed. Where did you go? What did you do? Add a photo if possible.

253

What are your responsibilities and duties?

254

What do you really want?

255

Think of a fairytale or story with a clear villain; now write a diary entry from their point of view. What happened that day? What do they want? How are they feeling? How did the pesky hero or heroine scupper their plans? Do they even think what they are doing is wrong?

256

What legacy do you want to leave to the world?

257

Which store would you choose for a free 10-minute trolley sweep? Where would you head to first? Write a list of all the things you would fill your trolley with.

258

If joy and happiness became the international currency of the world, do you think you would be rich or poor? What would make you richer?

259
What does the expression 'fortune favors the bold' mean to you?

260
What does 'satisfaction' mean to you?

261
Tell me about what can make you retreat from pursuing your goals and dreams?

262
Write a 10 years later update about one of your favorite fictional characters. What has happened to them since the happily ever after?

263
Tell me about one of the most daring things you have ever done.

264

Make a list of all the delicious foods you love to eat but wish they could magically be as beneficial to you as eating fruit and vegetables.

265

Think of a situation or person that is making you feel angry, sad or frustrated. Now scream, shout or roar as loud as you can into a pillow or cushion. Get it all out. Report back to journal.

266

Tell me about any acts of kindness you have received. How do you feel when someone does something kind for you?

Today turn envy into inspiration, by thinking about someone you feel envious of. Create a list of all the things you feel jealous about; is it their appearance, material possessions, lifestyle, personality traits, experiences, achievements etc?

Now with 10 being the most important and 1 the least, go through the list and for each one rate from 1 to 10 on how important (honestly) each point would be to improving your overall happiness. When rating them go a little bit deeper, for example are you really jealous of their expensive car because you want the exact same one? Or is it because you are actually envious of the fact that they have the money to spend on an expensive car?

For the points you rated highly take some time to write out some ways you too could have what they have but in your own individual way.

Some examples could be:
- They have confidence to spare: Push your boundaries; try new things to increase your self-confidence.
- They have a great social life: Put yourself in a position to meet lots of new potential friends such as joining a class or a team.
- They always look great: Make more of an effort with your appearance, wear your best, try a new style and improve your health & fitness levels.
- They have achieved so much: Although it may not always seem like it, underneath it all they were paddling hard like a swan. They had a goal and worked hard towards it over time. So decide on an achievement you want to accomplish and start paddling.
- They were born into money: Yes they may have been lucky enough to be born into money, but that money came from somewhere. At some point in their family history someone worked hard to create the wealth. So use them as motivation to work hard and know the money you make will feel twice as valuable because you earned it.

268

Tell me about the next big step you are going to take towards your dreams.

269

Write a day in the life from the perspective of a park bench. What does it see? Who sits on it? What are their stories? What changes around it over time?

270

Create a list of significant world events that have happened in your lifetime. Add a couple of images.

271

Which 5 famous or influential people would you like to be friends with and why? Where would you hang out?

272

In your journal draw something from your home or a view from a window. No judging, no erasing the lines. Just draw, sketch or doodle it. No skipping this prompt if your journal is lined, draw anyway.

"Don't screw up your drawings. If I wanted a picture perfect drawing, I would of asked you to pick up a camera not a pencil. Everyone's drawing style is special."
Mrs Harrison, one of my favorite schoolteachers.

273

List all the places you are grateful for having visited. Add some images if possible.

274

We all know our self confidence only grows when we expand our comfort zones, so tell me about a time when you pushed your boundaries and felt rewarded with a boost of self confidence afterwards. Now write down at least 5 things you could do to earn more confidence.

275

What do you want people to know you for? What do you want your 'thing' to be and why?

276

Combine one prompt from each column to create a plot-line for a short story.

	A	B	C
1	In India	a magazine editor with a passion for 1950's glamour	is mistakenly entered into the Olympics.
2	In Spain	an office worker with dreams of opening a diner where the staff wear roller skates	accidentally ends up on a stage in front of 10,000 people.
3	In a world with no electricity	one of the most famous people in the world	is magically transported into a cartoon world.
4	In a world where using the internet is illegal	a fairy with a fiery temper	shares a passionate kiss.
5	After finding $1 million cash	a shop mannequin	finds a magic lamp and is granted only one wish as the genie is in a bad mood.
6	After waking up as someone of the opposite sex	a sailor	finds themselves working with their idol.

277

Tell me about an occasion/event/moment that exceeded your expectations.

278

If you were to be magically turned into an animal, which would you choose & why?

279

Tell me about a time when you lost your temper. What was it about?

280

Tell me about a person who always makes you feel better.

281

Tell me what does 'home' mean to you?

In order to be irreplaceable, one must always be different

Coco Chanel

Life can be broken down into the following 10 areas:

1. Family
2. Health & wellbeing
3. Spirituality & faith
4. Career & finances
5. Love life
6. Social life
7. Creativity & self-expression
8. Personal interests
9. Self-exploration
10. Learning

Thinking about your life, rate each area from 1-10 (10 being perfect). Where do you see opportunities for growth? In your journal, free write about how you could improve them.

Then for each area you want to improve the most, write down at least one clear action you could take. Possible suggestions to help you grow in multiple areas at once could be:

Getting an additional part time job would increase your income (finances), allow you to acquire new skills (career & learning) and make new friends (social life).

Joining an art class would allow you to explore your inner artist (creativity & self expression), meet new people (social life) and discover new techniques (learning).

Going to the gym or a yoga studio (health & wellbeing) with a friend once a week (social life).

Note: Whenever you are offered a new opportunity which you might normally turn down because "I just don't have the time", "that's just not my kind of thing" or "I wouldn't be any good at it" take the time to ask yourself "which of the 10 life areas could it help me grow in?"

283

Write a day in the life from the perspective of a crystal chandelier above a private secluded seated area in an exclusive 5 star hotel lobby, popular with the rich and famous. What does it see? What secrets does it know?

284

Tell me about a time when everything went your way.

285

Create your alter ego. What would their name be? Write a list of personality traits you would like them to have. What would their personal style be like? How would they carry themselves? In what situations do you think having an alter ego would be useful?

Some famous examples:

Norma Jean Baker	Marilyn Monroe
Stefani Germanotta	Lady Gaga
Tara Leigh Patrick	Carmen Electra
Reginald Kenneth Dwight	Elton John
Maurice Joseph Micklewhite	Michael Caine
Shawn Carter	Jay Z
Katheryn Elizabeth Hudson	Katy Perry
Lizzie Grant	Lana Del Rey
Heather Renee Sweet	Dita Von Teese
Eileen Regina Edwards	Shania Twain
Margaret Hyra	Meg Ryan
Alicia Moore	Pink
Mark Sinclair Vincent	Vin Diesel
Eric Bishop	Jamie Foxx
Walter Willis	Bruce Willis

286

What is your most treasured family memory from the past year/3 years/5 years?

287

What aspects of your job do you enjoy? Big and small. If you are between jobs what will you enjoy about being employed or about creating your own opportunity?

288

What are you in denial about?

289

With no limitations or inhibitions complete the following statement in as much vivid detail as you and your pen can handle: My biggest dream is to...

290

Write a short story about a fictional spy mission you and your team went on. What was your mission objective? Who were you working for and against? What exciting and glamorous locations were you based? What didn't go to plan? Did you complete your objective?

291

Tell me as much as you can about a special person to you who has passed away. What did they enjoy doing? Where did they work? What did they teach you? How did they make you feel? Add a photo if you can.

292

If you had the ability to influence the minds of others for 24 hours what would you do and why?

293

Tell me about a time your first impression or assumption about a person or situation was completely wrong.

294

List your favorite actors & actresses with their best roles.

295

What do you think the secrets or keys to a happy life are?

296

My ideal body would be...

297

In the middle of the night you are woken up by a loud hammering sound coming from beneath your bed. You push back the bed and notice for the first time a golden handle attached to a circular trapdoor in the floorboards.

As you pull open the trapdoor your room is filled with daylight. As the trapdoor stands open you can see the top of a ladder but cannot see the bottom as it a long way down. You see a note nailed onto the inside of the door that reads... (Continue the story)

298

Tell me about a time when you laughed so hard you couldn't breathe or when you could not stop laughing at a really inappropriate time.

299

If you could choose, which era would you have liked to have been born into and why?

300

In detail plan a flash back party based on your childhood or teenage years. Complete with the types of party food you used to enjoy, music from the time and expected dress code from the era.

Or in detail, plan a themed party based on a movie, book or TV show. Decorate according to theme and require all those attending to wear suitable attire.

Note: If you throw a party (even just for yourself – lots of fun, you get to eat party food and dance without a care in the world) report back to journal complete with photos.

301

List your favorite musicians, bands and songs.

302

What qualities do you admire about yourself?

303

In detail write about how you would like people to feel after interacting with you.

304

Write a poem about the first thing which enters your mind after you read this prompt.

305

Tell me in detail about a time when you visited somewhere special.

306

What would you do if you had the super hero ability to fly for 24 hours?

307

What do you think people's first impressions of you are? What would you like it to be?

308

Tell me about some of the reasons you are grateful about the country where you live.

309
Who do you admire and why?

310
From head to toe (kindly) rate the different areas of your body. Which do you like? Which areas could do with a tune up? This includes the health of your heart. Write a list of a few realistic actions (big or small) you could do to help make improvements. Some examples to help improve your health and fitness could be:

- Going to the gym or exercising at home at least twice a week.
- Making an effort to walk for at least 20 minutes a day.
- For every 3 biscuits you take out of the cookie jar put 1 back (that is already a 33% calorie saving).
- Eat more fruit & vegetables.
- During the commercial breaks on TV you could jog on the spot/do some squats/jumping jacks/pretend to jump rope.
- When you are getting ready in the morning turn up your favorite music and dance away like no one is watching.
- At night take the time to stretch before bed to improve your flexibility, etc.

Then in your journal make the following agreement with yourself:

"I promise to take the small and manageable action(s) of (personal action of choice) to help improve my overall health and wellbeing because I deserve it. I am also doing this for the sake of (those you care for and care for you)."

Signed...

(Note: Please consult with your Doctor/Physician before beginning any exercise program.)

311
Write a day in the life of someone you admire (real or fictional).

312
Tell me about a time when you tried something new.

313
What would you do if you had the ability to read minds for 24 hours?

314
What are some of the biggest hurdles standing in your way right now?

315
Create a list of services different companies provide that you are grateful for. Such as the internet, electricity, heating, clean water etc. Why do you feel grateful for them? How different would your life be if you did not have easy access to them for 30 days?

316
Tell me about the biggest decision you made today/this week/this month/this year.

317

Imagine waking up 10 years in the future doing the same things you are doing today. Is there anything you could do now differently in the present that would make you happier and improve your quality of life in the future?

318

In your journal write an article for a magazine or blog about a subject you are passionate about and interested in. Sharing what you know about the article subject with the reader. Mind map or list some potential topics first.

If you are struggling to think of a topic ask yourself "what advice do people come to me for?" or "what is it that I know that could benefit others?" Are you the person who gives good advice about gadgets, relationships, money, creative projects, fashion? Write your article about 'your thing' (everyone has at least one).

319

Create a list of things you enjoyed as a child. Add a photo of you as a child.

320

What 10 fun & ridiculous laws would you pass if you were King/ Queen or President?

321

Tell me about something you know you can do better than most people.

And the time came when the risk to remain tight in a bud was more painful than the risk it took to blossom

Anais Nin

322

Tell me about one of your favorite memories from the past year.

323

What would really help you right now?

324

I am a great...

325

In as much detail write about what can you hear, smell, see and taste right now?

326

On a double page spread write your Mother's (or Mother figure's) name in the centre of the left page and your Father's (or Father figure's) in the center of the right page.

Now mind map out from each name their qualities, values, skills, talents, nature, habits, temperaments, lessons they taught you and their style, etc.

Then circle the qualities you inherited and underline the ones you would like to have yourself. Add a photo of them.

327

Invent a national holiday celebrating you. What would it be called? What food would be eaten? What sort of decorations would people put up and what would they wear? What traditions would people do on your day?

328

Set a timer for 15 minutes, now for the full 15 minutes do not stop writing. Whatever thoughts cross your mind write them down, do not censor yourself or worry about spelling and punctuation. Just clear all of the mental clutter out onto the paper. After the 15 minutes relax and reward yourself.

329

Tell me about a few things that have happened over the past 30 days that you are grateful for.

330

What moves you?

331

What does 'having purpose' mean to you?

332

Tell me about a time when you visited somewhere special you had never been before. Pretend you are there again and in as much detail write about what you can see, hear, smell, and taste as if you are there again. Remember through your senses.

333

Create a list of things you enjoyed as a teenager. Add a photograph of teenage you, the more embarrassing the better.

334

Create a list of things you enjoy doing on your own.

335

What are you most excited about right now? Why?

336

What is your favorite season? Make a list of all the things you love about it. Go through all your senses, what do you like to see, feel, smell, taste and hear?

337
What motivates you?

338
What do you wish you were bold or brave enough to do?

339
Think about one of your greatest fears; now write a short story about someone over coming that fear.

340
Tell me about a 'wow' or 'oh yeah' moment in your life. When you came to a realization and something made complete sense. What happened? Where were you? What did you realize/learn?

341
I am a self-confessed...

342
What act of kindness have you recently seen in person or in the media that has rekindled your faith in people?

343
I am grateful for my healthy heart because...

344
Tell me about one of the biggest decisions you have ever made.

345
Imagine you were told the world was going to end in 7 days time.
Tell me about how would you want to spend those 7 days? Doing
what, where and with who?

Action: Choose one thing and do it this week.

Combine one prompt from each column to create a
plot-line for a short story.

	A	B	C
1	During a bank robbery	a CEO of a multi billion dollar company	accidentally discovers an ancient temple full of treasures and danger.
2	After finding a lost teddy bear	a resourceful cheerleader	has to face their fear of heights.
3	After being followed home by a lost dog	an admired TV personality	has to face their fear of open water.
4	While on their way home from a hard days work	a jeweler with an eye for detail	must base jump from a skyscraper to avoid capture.
5	After finding somebody's wallet	a country and western singer	makes a deal with a wizard to receive one wish but must exchange it for something of the same value and meaning.
6	After waking up to discover everything they touch turns to solid gold	a hungry talking tiger with a British accent	must pet sit a baby Rhino for a week.

347

Tell me about an embarrassing moment in your life that is now funny looking back on it.

348

If everyone abandoned your city or town for 24 hours how would you spend the day? The entire city is your playground for the 24 hours.

349

Tell me about some recent memories that make you smile.

350

List as many simple pleasures you enjoy as you can.

351

What does 'having momentum' mean to you?

352

Tell me about a time when you failed at something multiple times before you eventually succeeded. How did you achieve your goal? How did it feel?

Are there any situations in your life now that could benefit from you being as persistent?

353

Write about a memorable day on one side of your journal; now write about the day in opposites on the opposite page. Turn any descriptions upside down; night is day, hot is cold, rain is sunshine, male is female, up is down, happy is sad, black is white, blunt is sharp etc.

Alternatively you can 'opposite' a page from one of your favorite books. Note: Keep as a surreal source of inspiration.

354

Where were you this time last year/5 years ago/10 years ago?

355

Make up a situation where you performed an amazingly heroic act. Write out the speech you would give to the media at a press conference after.

356

Write a list of all the things you wanted to be when you grew up. Now think about how you can make one of them come true for one day. Did you want to be a dancer? Join a dance class for a day. A footballer? Join a football training session. A vet? Volunteer at an animal sanctuary for a day.

Work through your ideas in your journal and then choose one. Research and plan how you can make it happen. Report back to your journal when you have done it.

Extra: Plan and host a 'when I grow up' party where your guests attend dressed up as what they wanted to be when they were younger. Report back to journal.

357

If someone has read this far into your journal, what would you like them to have learned from you and why?

358

What advice or pep talk would you like to give yourself?

359
How are you feeling today?

360
List over 50 practical, creative and ridiculous uses for a one of the following:

A pencil
A vase
A used lightbulb
A shipping container
A piece of copier paper
A used book
A car tyre
A shed
A paper clip

361
Some of the ways I have benefited from journal writing are...

362
Write a fake acceptance speech for an award such as an Oscar, Grammy, Noble Peace Prize or for any award you would really love to win.

Who would you want to thank? What does it mean to you? Would you start crying? Would the host need to drag you off the stage to stop you talking? Who would be in the crowd? What would you be wearing?

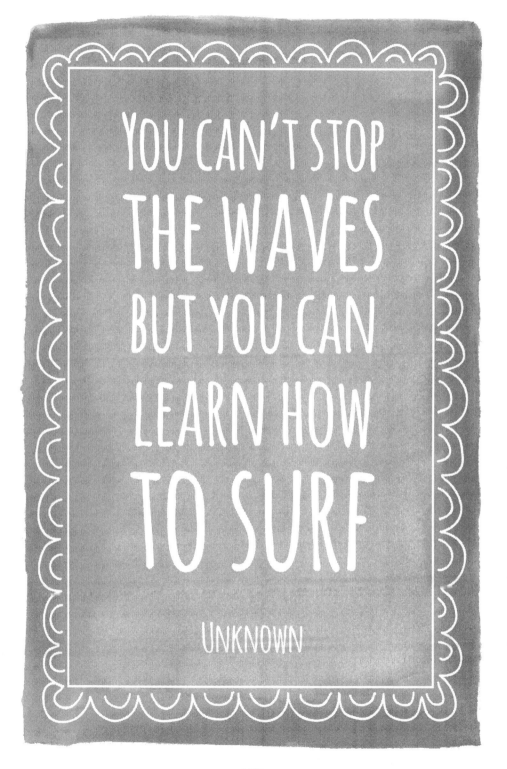

YOU CAN'T STOP THE WAVES BUT YOU CAN LEARN HOW TO SURF

UNKNOWN

363

If 'the bank of life' appeared in your town for only one day and offered you the following:

- Take 10 years off of your life to become one of the most attractive people in the world.
- Take 10 years off of your life to become incredibly intelligent.
- Take 10 years off of your life to become a millionaire.
- Take 10 years off of your life to meet and marry the love of your life.
- Take 10 years off of your life in exchange for international fame.
- Take 10 years off of your life to be one the best at what you do for a living.
- Take 20 years off of your life to complete 100 items on your bucket list.
- Take 20 years off of your life to become a billionaire.
- Add 10 years to your life in exchange for 5 of your greatest memories.
- Add 10 years to your life in exchange for having never met someone you care about.

Which ones would you cash in or be tempted by and why? Which would you refuse and why? Would you even be alive today if you had entered this bank as a teenager?

364

Tell me about a few things that have happened over the last 364 days that you are grateful for.

365

What are you looking forward to
about the next 365 days?

Can I take this opportunity to say **congratulations** for we have now reached the end of our year-long journaling journey and a massive thank you for reading my first book and I really hope it has helped you in some way.

The good news is all the prompts in this book can be used again and again, year after year. Plus over the course of a year we change so much and there is always so much more of you to unearth (maybe some even shinier diamonds). So why not go around again? Maybe this time with a friend or family member? Let's do it...

Use this space to add any additional journaling prompts...

147

The Weekly Actions

Week 1.

Create a happy memories jar. Any empty glass jar with a screw lid will do. Keep slips of paper small enough to fold up and put into the jar next to your happy memories jar.

Throughout the year note any great moments or events and add them to the jar (as well as noting them in your journal). Then at the end of the year you can tip them out and read to relive the memories or for those days when you are in need of a boost. Spend a few moments going through the memories to cheer yourself up.

Then after the year keep the jar on a bookshelf or in a box labeled with the year to build up a collection.

Week 2.

Call or text someone you have not spoken to in too long. Report back to journal.

Week 3.

Send a postcard or a handwritten letter to yourself from wherever you are. When it arrives tape the postcard into your journal or glue the envelope in with the letter inside.

Week 4.

Choose one of the photography prompts & report back to your journal with your favorite photograph.

Week 5.

Create a Bucket List Bank. Set up a separate savings account and put in a percentage of your earnings or save money into an unused jar with a screw lid and dedicate the funds to paying towards completing something from your bucket list.

Decorate the outside of the jar with some images of the places and experiences you want. Having the images on the outside will make it less tempting to 'dip' into.

Also keep it away from the front door to prevent the temptation to 'borrow' from it when you fancy going for a coffee or want to buy a magazine etc. Keep an eye out for any offers/discounts related to the things from you list.

Week 6.

Watch an uplifting movie or a thought-provoking documentary you have been meaning to watch this week. Report back to journal.

Week 7.

Plant some seeds this week and stick the empty packet into your journal. Over the next few weeks and months add photos or draw sketches in your journal of their progress as they grow.

Week 8.

Go somewhere different. Somewhere you have never been. Take your journal and note your new surroundings, the sights, the sounds, the smells and the people.

Week 9.

Do something that helps someone else. It could be helping with chores around the house, offering help to a neighbor, donating something to a cause you believe in, volunteering, helping someone with a project etc. Report back to journal.

Week 10.

Give a child you know a camera and let them take photographs of anything they find interesting, stick a few of your favorites into your journal. Or give them a blank sheet of paper and some pens/crayons/paints and stick their works of art into your journal.

Week 11.

Choose one of the photography prompts & report back to your journal with your favorite photograph.

Week 12.

Write and post a handwritten letter to someone. Report back to journal. Extra: Ask them to write back to you & stick in their letter when it arrives.

Week 13.

This week at a magazine stand go to where your usual favorite magazine is, now take 3 big side steps to the left or right. Now buy the first magazine that stands out the most to you. Hopefully it should be about a subject or for a demographic you do not normally read about. Report back to journal about anything new you have learned.

Week 14.

Be Royal this week by following the rule 'never complain, never explain'. Do not speak negatively about anyone or anything (if you do quickly follow up with a positive) and do not explain your actions to anyone unnecessarily.

Make a real effort with your appearance this week as if your life is of interest to the world media. Dress to impress by wearing your nicest clothes and after you get dressed do not forget to put on your invisible crown.

Your invisible crown will help you walk and sit with better posture because you do not want to let it fall from your head by walking too fast, by sitting hunched over or slouching. Report back to journal.

Week 15.

Leave a note inside a book at the library or bookshop giving the finder a compliment, an uplifting quote or a positive word of advice you have found useful. Or if you are feeling really generous (& can afford it) leave a $5 note inside.

Even better leave it in a book that you love, a book that has maybe helped you or inside a book you think a person would pick up when they are looking for help or hope. Your note or gift could be enough to help someone through a tough time. Report back to journal.

Wook 16.

Choose one of the photography prompts & report back to your journal with your favorite photograph.

Week 17.

Make an effort to make conversation with someone different this week or help make someone new feel really welcome. Extra: Say good morning to at least 3 strangers every morning. Report back to journal.

Week 18.

Can you think of someone who would benefit from an act of kindness? What could you do for them? What would cheer them up? Do it. Report back to journal.

Week 19.

Go on a staycation by being a tourist in your hometown. Spend a day doing 'touristy' things. Even go to the tourist information office to ask them for any recommendations. You might even learn something new about your hometown. Pretend everything is new to you.

Keep all the maps, tickets and leaflets from the day and stick them into your journal along with any explanations about how you spent the day. Note: Stick in an envelope to keep any photos of your staycation together.

Week 20.

Send someone a thank you note. Report back to journal.

Week 21.

Everyday this week stand in front of a mirror and out loud say 5 things you like about yourself. After each one, hold eye contact with yourself and smile, or maybe even give yourself a cheeky wink. How did the exercise make you feel? Report back to journal.

Note: From now on try to create the habit of thinking or saying out loud one thing you like about yourself anytime you look into a mirror or see your reflection.

Week 22.

For at least one day this week (more the better) record how you spend your 24 hours. In your journal write down on the left hand side of the page the times below, one for each line. Then for each hour write down what you are doing or what you have done.

05:00 ....

06:00 ....

07:00 ....

08:00 ....

09:00 ....

10:00 ....

11:00 ....

12:00 ....

13:00 ....

14:00 ....

15:00 ....

16:00 ....

17:00 ....

18:00 ....

19:00 ....

20:00 ....

21:00 ....

22:00 ....

23:00 ....

00:00 ....

01:00 ....

02:00 ....

03:00 ....

04:00 ....

Are you happy with how you spent your 24 hours today? Did you make enough time for yourself, personal projects, family & friends? How many hours did you spend online and watching TV? What else could you be doing?

Note: For extra detail, imagine you are the subject of a scientific study and record everything. What did you wear? Eat? Buy? Do? Who did you interact with? Even take a photo of whatever you are doing every 60 minutes.

I discovered this technique in college; I think to encourage us to watch less daytime TV and to study more. I have since discovered a great book called '168 Hours: You Have More Time Than You Think by Laura Vanerkam' about getting more out of your 168 hours each week.

Week 23.
This week schedule in some 'you-time'. To do something you enjoy like going to the movies, shopping, going for a walk, going to the gym, playing a sport, yoga, catching up on a book, eating ice cream while watching TV. Anything you enjoy doing but do not make the time for often enough. Report back to journal.

Week 24.
Think of a person you admire, real or fictional. Spend the week living as they would. Ask yourself "what would (blank) do in this situation?" Report back to journal.

Week 25.
Assess your health by booking yourself in for a check up with your Doctor this week. Report back to journal.

"Prevention is better than a cure."
Proverb

Week 26.

Assess your fitness levels this week by booking yourself in for a personal training session. It could be traditional gym training, running, swimming, yoga, pilates, martial arts etc, whatever appeals to you.

Remember to note in your journal anything they recommend you should work on & take advantage of any introductory discounts they offer if you feel they would help you stay motivated.

If you think of fitness as something only the vain and time-rich can indulge in or you don't like exercise because none of your previous efforts have worked, shift your mindset and think of it as something you are doing for the sake of your heart and not your waistline.

Instead of running to the mirror to look at your stomach and sighing because you have not got flat defined abs like an athlete after only one 30-minute workout (who hasn't done that?). Know that the 30 minutes has been beneficial for your heart and by focusing on improving the health of your heart often, before long without realizing it your body will soon take shape almost like an added bonus.

You will feel better, look better and have more energy.

Note: Please consult with your Doctor/Physician before beginning any exercise program.

FOCUS ON
WHAT YOUR
BODY CAN DO,
NOT ON WHAT
IT LOOKS LIKE

UNKNOWN

Week 27.

This week become a 'guerilla gardener' by secretly planting a colorful flower or seeds somewhere neglected or dull. Report back to journal.

Week 28.

Choose one of the photography prompts & report back to your journal with your favorite photograph.

Week 29.

Schedule a 'digital detox day'. No internet, no TV, no movies, no gaming, no email, no apps & no texting. You can use your phone to make actual phone calls if necessary.

After report back to journal how it felt not relying on technology for one day, did you find it frustrating or liberating?

Week 30.

Send someone a gift without them knowing it is from you. Report back to journal.

Week 31.

Make the time one night this week to sit under the stars with a hot drink or look out of a window with all of your lights switched off and just take the time to look at the stars and night sky until you finish your drink (or longer). Report back to journal.

Week 32.

Take your journal to a busy hotel and sit in the lobby or bar. Write about all the people who are coming and going. Note their style, how they interact with each other, what types of drinks did they order, what are they wearing? Where do you think they are from? How do you think they know each other?

If you can't make it to a hotel go to a busy train station or coffee shop.

Note: This can be good source for fictional characters.

Week 33.

Sort out your wardrobe/closet. Resist the temptation to pull everything out at once. As this can result in a mini emotional crisis on the floor while you are knee high in t-shirts, shoes and jeans screaming "why did I even bother starting this!"

Prepare with a supply of your favorite snacks, put on some music or a movie and declare your room a no go zone for anyone else until you are finished. As you work through each section divide clothing and shoes into 5 groups:

1. Keep me
2. Store me
3. Sell or Swap me
4. Donate me
5. Recycle me.

Keep me: In your closet/wardrobe group your keep me clothes first by color, from left to right: dark to light. Then within each color from left to right start with work wear, evening-wear, smart casual, casual & chill-out clothes. Or group your clothes by function first, left to right: Work wear, evening-wear, smart casual, casual & chill out. Then within each group order by color, dark to light.

When you hang your keep me clothes back up, hang the closest hanger facing the wrong way. So in 3 months time you will see which items of clothing you have not touched within 3 months.

Store me: The seasonal items (beach hats, bikinis, board shorts, big wooly jumpers, scarves, gloves) can be stored away for the next time their season comes around.

Sell or Swap me: Sell your unwanted clothing to a second hand clothes merchant, sell them yourself online, rent a market stall for a day to run your very own pop up vintage store, sell at a garage/car boot sale etc. Swap clothes with friends and family or look for a local 'swishing' event.

Donate me: Send to a charity shop, find a clothes bank or arrange for a charity to collect from you.

Recycle me: For clothes that have had their day, put them into a clothes recycling bank so the materials can be used to make something else.

Shoes: After playing a game of find the pairs, use elastic bands to keep the pairs together.

Report back to journal how the process went. Did you rediscover any forgotten favorites? Did you find any items of clothing difficult to part with based on memories? How does it feel having a tidier more organized closet/wardrobe space?

Note: Carry out this exercise in your underwear and try on every piece of clothing as you go and have a quick look in the mirror. Does it still fit? Does it suit you any more? Also don't forget to take before and after photos of your closet space.

Week 34.
This week schedule in a daily 20-minute wish walk. On your own go for a walk without listening to any music and spend the time imagining you have all the things you want. When any other thoughts pop up simply dismiss and replace with another wish.

Note: If you cannot spare 20 minutes a day you can fit this into a busy schedule by wish walking whenever you are walking anywhere alone. Report back to journal.

Week 35.
Host a 3-course meal by candlelight. Use your best plates and cutlery, dress to impress & play some music. Plan the details in your journal. Enjoy the food and the time with your partner, family, friends or your own company. Report back to journal.

Week 36.
Reenact a childhood photo. Find a photograph of yourself as a child and pose in the exact same position with the same facial expression wearing clothes of similar color and style. Try and take the photo in the same location or somewhere like it. Stick the photos into your journal side by side.

If you have a cat or dog you could reenact a photo of you with them as a puppy or kitten. Even better, find a group photo from your childhood such as a family portrait and get them involved too.

Note: If you have a young family you could do this once a year to see how much everyone changes, year to year.

Week 37.
Call someone up for a catch up. Report back to journal.

Week 38.
This week when meeting new people, try greeting them like you would an old friend. Warm smile, eye contact and keep your arms uncrossed. Pretend like you have known them for years. Report back to journal.

Week 39.
De-clutter a space in your home. Put on some music, prepare some snacks and remember to do it gradually in sections. Take before and after photos. Report back to journal.

Week 40.
Choose one of the photography prompts & report back to your journal with your favorite photograph.

Week 41.

Live this week as your alter ego from prompt No. 285. Do, say, wear, walk, eat, talk and work like they would. If a stranger asks your name, you could even use your alter ego's name. In every situation ask yourself "what would (alter ego's name) do?" Report back to journal.

Week 42.

Take a nature walk somewhere you can get some fresh air and clear out the mental cobwebs, such as going to a park, a beach or lake etc. Photograph or sketch any interesting views or discoveries on your adventure. Keep and eye out for things to tape into your journal such as leaves or flowers.

How was it? What did you see? What thoughts came up during your walk?

Week 43.

In an elevator this week face the opposite direction to everyone else. Hold your ground as if it is perfectly normal for the 30 second ride. How empowered and bold did this simple act make you feel? Report back to journal.

Note: If you find it too challenging you can look at your phone or a magazine just remain a rebel and face the wrong way.

HAPPINESS
OFTEN SNEAKS IN
THROUGH A DOOR
YOU DIDN'T KNOW
YOU LEFT OPEN

JOHN BARRYMORE

Week 44.

Schedule in some rest and relaxation for yourself. You could get a massage, a facial, a manicure/pedicure, book into a hotel for a night, catch up on a book in the bath, switch off your phone and watch a movie etc. In your journal work through some ideas, choose one and make it happen. Report back to journal after.

Note: If it seems too expensive to go to a spa for a massage or beauty treatments, beauty schools & colleges offer discounted treatments as a way for the students to gain experience while being fully supervised. So you are getting a professional service for a fraction of the price of a spa.

Week 45.

Sign up for a part time or one-day class for a subject you enjoy or you have always wanted to learn more about. Report back to journal.

Week 46.

When in conversation this week practice your listening skills. Do not simply wait for the other person to finish talking so you can start. Listen to what they are saying; repeat back keywords or phrases for them to expand on. You are developing an important skill while they are feeling noticed and actually heard. Report back to journal.

Note: Avoid making conversations about you, for example try not to say "I know what you are talking about because something similar happened to me when…" because that will only take the attention away from the other person.

Week 47.

This week schedule in a daily 20-minute gratitude walk. On your own go for a walk without listening to any music and spend the time thinking about all the things you are grateful for about your life and the rest of the world. If any other thoughts pop up just dismiss them and replace by thinking of something else you are grateful for.

Note: If you cannot spare 20 minutes a day you can fit this into a busy schedule by gratitude walking whenever you are walking anywhere alone. Report back to journal.

Week 48.

Research to find any charities that organize one of the activities from your bucket list in exchange for you raising sponsorship money. For example sponsored skydives, mountain climbing etc. Sign up. Ask friends, family, work colleagues, local shops, local newspaper, radio stations etc to sponsor you.

Use your bucket list bank fund to sponsor yourself. Document your research and progress in your journal.

Week 49.

Take a walk around your neighborhood or town. Write everything down or take photos to describe things in further detail later. Pretend you are a location scout for a movie. Then in your journal write about the location as if it is the setting in the opening chapter of a book or movie, set the scene.

Week 50.
Plant a tree. Report back to journal with a photo.

Week 51.
Create a self-portrait of yourself. It could be a sketch, a doodle, a cartoon, a painting, a photograph or a collage etc. Completely your choice, do not be judgmental or critical of it, just enjoy the process. Report back to journal.

Week 52.
You and your journal are going to a busy restaurant alone together. You are going to be that mysterious and interesting person who has the confidence to dine alone to work on their important project. Take this timeout to reflect over your journal(s).

Write about the food, the service, your surroundings and about the people and their interactions.

With any luck you might be treated like royalty as the staff could assume you are a food critic. If anyone asks, simply say you are a writer. After dessert, over coffee or tea while still sitting in the restaurant, write about how this experience has made you feel. Empowered & brave?

Use this space to add any additional weekly actions...

THE PHOTOGRAPHY PROMPTS

For a weeklong photography challenge choose a prompt word from the list below and keep your camera or camera phone with you and keep an eye out for any opportunities to take as many interesting photographs of the subject as you can.

Interpretation of the prompt word is totally up to you. Then report back to your journal with your favourite 1-3 photographs.

Happy snapping!

Shadows
Vivid
Reflection
Texture
Silhouette
Family
Strangers
Home
Away
Up high
Down low
Motion
Calm
Gentle
Hard
New beginnings
Adventure
Love
Space
Secrets
Flight
Mystery

Strong
Regal
Fragile
Up close
From a far
Monochrome
Cheerful
Majestic
Flowers
Water
Hustle & Bustle
Portrait
Landscape
Scary
Out of focus
Wild
Old
Playful
Dangerous
Lazy
Creative
Shimmer

If you prefer you could use the list as inspiration to draw, paint or collage the subjects into your journal. Choose whichever creative medium you enjoy the most.

Use this space to add any additional photography prompts...

THE QUOTES

ADVENTURE

The cave you fear to enter holds the treasure you seek.
Joseph Campbell

I am not afraid of storms for I am learning how to sail my ship.
Louisa May Alcott

One can never consent to creep when one feels the impulse to soar.
Helen Keller

Where there's a will, there's a way.
Old English Proverb

We live in a wonderful world that is full of beauty, charm and
adventure. There is no end to the adventures that we can have if
only we seek them with our eyes open.
Jawaharlal Nehru

One does not discover new lands without consenting to lose sight of
the shore for a very long time.
Andre Gide

It is not the easy or convenient life for which I search, but life lived
to the edge of all that I may be.
Mary Anne Radmacher

The biggest adventure you can take is to live the life of your dreams.
Oprah Winfrey

A ship in harbor is safe - but that is not what ships are for.
John A. Shedd

There is no passion to be found playing small - in settling for a life
that is less than the one you are capable of living.
Nelson Mandela

The trouble is, if you don't risk anything, you risk even more.
Erica Jong

Do not follow where the path may lead.
Go, instead, where there is no path and leave a trail.
Ralph Waldo Emerson

We must dare, and dare again, and go on daring.
Georges Jacques Danton

It is better to err on the side of daring than the side of caution.
Alvin Toffler

It is not because life is difficult that we do not dare.
Life is difficult because we do not dare.
Seneca

The world is a book and those who do not travel read only one page.
Saint Augustine of Hippo

AGE

Years wrinkle the skin, but lack of enthusiasm wrinkles the soul.
N.V.Peale

We don't stop playing because we grow old;
we grow old because we stop playing.
George Bernard Shaw

Forty is the old age of youth; fifty is the youth of old age.
Victor Hugo

You know you are getting old when the
candles cost more than the cake.
Bob Hope

A major advantage of age is learning to accept
people without passing judgment.
Liz Carpenter

Age is no barrier. It's a limitation you put on your mind.
Unknown

A man among children will be long a child,
a child among men will soon be a man.
Unknown

Age appears to be best in four things – old wood best to burn,
old wine to drink, old friends to trust, and old authors to read.
Alonso Of Aragon

Age does not diminish the extreme disappointment of
having a scoop of ice cream fall from the cone.
Jim Fiebig

Age is case of mind over matter. If you don't mind, it don't matter.
Satchel Paige

ANGER

For every minute you are angry
you lose sixty seconds of happiness.
Ralph Waldo Emerson

Man should forget his anger before he lies down to sleep.
Gandhi

You will not be punished for your anger;
you will be punished by your anger.
Buddha

You can no more win a war than you can win an earthquake.
Jeannette Rankin

Peace begins with a smile.
Mother Teresa

A man is about as big as the things that make him angry.
Winston Churchill

A woman can hide her love for 40 years,
but her disgust and anger not for one day.
Arab Proverb

An angry man is again angry with himself,
when he returns to reason.
Publilius Syrus

Anger is a thief who steals away even the nicest of moments.
Unknown

BEAUTY

Everything has its beauty, but not everyone sees it.
Confucius

A beautiful thing never gives so much pain
as does failing to hear and see it.
Michelangelo

Some people, no matter how old they get, never lose their beauty –
they merely move it from their faces into their hearts.
Martin Buxbaum

A beauty is a woman you notice; a charmer is one who notices you.
Adlai E Stevenson

Anyone who keeps the ability to see beauty never grows old.
Franz Kafka

Those who contemplate the beauty of the earth find reserves of
strength that will endure as long as life lasts.
Rachel Carson

Sometimes people are beautiful. Not in looks.
Not in what they say. Just in what they are.
Markus Zusak

Beauty comes from a life well lived. If you've lived well, your smile
lines are in the right places, and your frown lines aren't too bad,
what more do you need?
Jennifer Garner

CHANGE

The jump is so frightening between where I am, and where I want to
be. Because of all I may become, I will close my eyes and leap.
Mary Anne Radmacher

What you resist you become.
Taoist saying

You must be the change you wish to see in the world.
Mahatma Gandhi

If you don't like something, change it.
If you can't change it, change your attitude. Don't complain.
Maya Angelou

Progress is impossible without change, and those who cannot
change their minds cannot change anything.
George Bernard Shaw

Consider how hard it is to change yourself and you'll understand
what little chance you have in trying to change others.
Jacob M. Braude

Change the changeable, accept the unchangeable, and remove
yourself from the unacceptable.
Denis Waitley

The only difference between a rut and a grave is their dimensions.
Ellen Glasgow

CHEERFUL

Cheerfulness is the atmosphere under which all things thrive.
Jean Paul Richter

You've gotta dance like there's nobody watching,
Love like you'll never be hurt, Sing like there's nobody listening,
And live like it's heaven on earth.
William W. Purkey

Don't cry because it's over, smile because it happened.
Dr. Seuss

Life is a shipwreck, but we must not forget to sing in the lifeboats.
Voltaire

While there is a chance of the world getting through its troubles,
I hold that a reasonable man has to behave as though he were
sure of it. If at the end your cheerfulness is not justified,
at any rate you will have been cheerful.
H G Wells

My religion of life is always to be cheerful.
George Meredith

How can they say my life is not a success? Have I not for more
than 60 years got enough to eat and escaped being eaten?
Logan Pearsall Smith

When you dance, your purpose is not to get to a certain place
on the floor. It's to enjoy each step along the way.
Wayne Dyer

Life is a song - sing it.
Life is a game - play it.
Life is a challenge - meet it.
Life is a dream - realize it.
Life is a sacrifice - offer it.
Life is love - enjoy it.
Sai Baba

C O U R A G E

All our dreams can come true,
if we have the courage to pursue them.
Walt Disney

A life lived in fear is a life half lived.
Anonymous

Courage doesn't always roar. Sometimes courage is the quiet voice
at the end of the day, saying, "I will try again tomorrow."
Mary Anne Radmacher

It takes courage to grow up and turn out to be who you really are.
E.E. Cummings

Courage is what it takes to stand up and speak.
Courage is also what it takes to sit down and listen.
Winston Churchill

Success is never final. Failure is never fatal.
It's courage that counts.
John Wooden

Courage is being scared to death but saddling up anyway.
John Wayne

Courage is grace under pressure.
Ernest Hemingway

Courage is facing your fears. Stupidity is fearing nothing.
Todd Bellemare

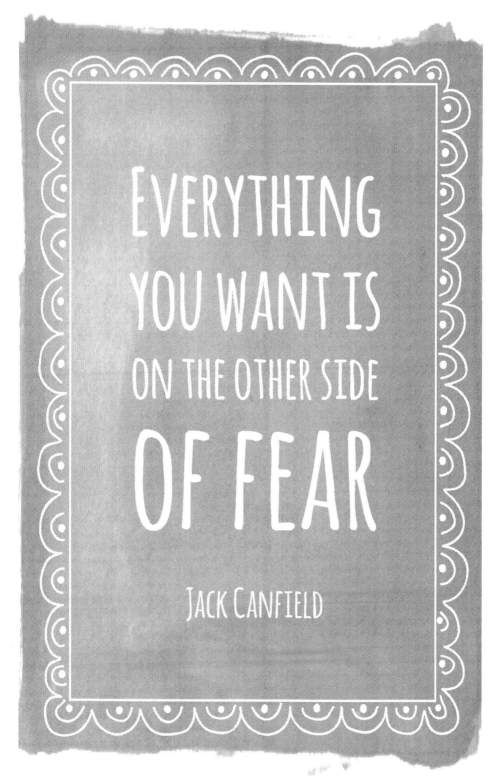

EVERYTHING YOU WANT IS ON THE OTHER SIDE OF FEAR

Jack Canfield

The most courageous act is still to think for yourself. Aloud.
Coco Chanel

Man cannot discover new oceans unless he has the
courage to lose sight of the shore.
Andre Gide

You gain strength, courage, and confidence by every experience
in which you really stop to look fear in the face.
You must do the thing which you think you cannot do.
Eleanor Roosevelt

Only those who will risk going too far can
possibly find out how far one can go.
T S Eliot

CREATIVITY

Imagination is more important than knowledge.
Albert Einstein

I like nonsense, it wakes up the brain cells.
Fantasy is a necessary ingredient in living.
Dr. Seuss

Every child is an artist.
The problem is how to remain an artist once he grows up.
Pablo Picasso

There is no doubt that creativity is the most important human
resource of all. Without creativity, there would be no progress,
and we would be forever repeating the same patterns.
Edward de Bono

Creativity is thinking up new things.
Innovation is doing new things.
Theodore Levitt

A new idea is delicate. It can be killed by a sneer or a yawn; it can be stabbed to death by a quip and worried to death by a frown on the right man's brow.
Charles Brower

It is better to have enough ideas for some of them to be wrong, than to be always right by having no ideas at all.
Edward de Bono

Creativity is inventing, experimenting, growing, taking risks, breaking rules, making mistakes, and having fun.
Mary Lou Cook

The world is but a canvas to the imagination.
Henry David Thoreau

Everyone who's ever taken a shower has had an idea. It's the person who gets out of the shower, dries off and does something about it who makes a difference.
Nolan Bushnell

Listen to anyone with an original idea, no matter how absurd it may sound at first. If you put fences around people, you get sheep. Give people the room they need.
William McKnight

Around here, however, we don't look backwards for very long. We keep moving forward, opening up new doors and doing new things, because we're curious... and curiosity keeps leading us down new paths.
Walt Disney

Ideas are like rabbits. You get a couple and learn how to handle them, and pretty soon you have a dozen.
John Steinbeck

If you hear a voice within you say, 'You cannot paint,' then by all
means paint, and that voice will be silenced.
Vincent van Gogh

Creativity is contagious. Pass it on.
Albert Einstein

An invasion of armies can be resisted,
but not an idea whose time has come.
Victor Hugo

To be creative means to be in love with life. You can be creative only
if you love life enough that you want to enhance its beauty, you
want to bring a little more music to it, a little more poetry to it,
a little more dance to it.
Osho

Creativity can solve almost any problem. The creative act, the
defeat of habit by originality, overcomes everything.
George Lois

Life is trying things to see if they work.
Ray Bradbury

Every artist writes his own autobiography.
Havelock Ellis

DEATH

As a well-spent day brings happy sleep,
so a life well spent brings happy death.
Leonardo Da Vinci

Even death is not to be feared by one who has lived wisely.
Buddha

The fear of death follows from the fear of life.
A man who lives fully is prepared to die at any time.
Mark Twain

If I think more about death than some other people,
it is probably because I love life more than they do.
Angelina Jolie

Dying can't be all that difficult,
up to now everyone has managed to do it.
Norman Mailer

A person starts dying when they stop dreaming.
Brian Williams

Do not fear death... only the unlived life.
You don't have to live forever; You just have to live.
Natalie Babbitt

EDUCATION

And where does magic come from?
I think that magic's in the learning.
Dar Williams

Education is when you read the fine print.
Experience is what you get if you don't.
Pete Seeger

To repeat what others have said requires education.
To challenge it requires brains.
Marry Pettibone Poole

Life is not divided into semesters. You don't get summers off and
very few employers are interested in helping you find yourself.
Bill Gates

The only true wisdom is knowing that you know nothing.
Socrates

There is no education like adversity.
Benjamin Disraeli

191

An education is what you have left after you
have forgotten all of the course content.
Unknown

FAMILY

A happy family is but an earlier heaven.
George Bernard Shaw

Family isn't about whose blood you have.
It's about who you care about.
Trey Parker and Matt Stone

You know the only people who are always sure about the proper
way to raise children? Those who've never had any.
Bill Cosby

Happiness is having a large, loving, caring,
close-knit family in another city.
George Burns

Always be nice to your children because they are the
ones who will choose your rest home.
Phyllis Diller

A boy becomes a man when he stops asking his
father for money and requests a loan.
Unknown

Home is not where you live, but where they understand you.
Christian Morganstern

Adults are always asking little kids what they want to be
when they grow up 'cause they're looking for ideas.
Paula Poundstone

A house divided against itself cannot stand.
Old English Proverb

Home is where you can say anything you please,
because nobody pays any attention to you anyway.
Joe Moore

A family is a place where minds come in contact with one another.
If these minds love one another the home will be as beautiful as a
flower garden. But if these minds get out of harmony with one
another it is like a storm that plays havoc with thee.
Buddha

A parent is a banker provided by nature.
Proverb

A house is made of walls and beams;
a home is built with love and dreams.
Unknown

Home is a place you grow up wanting to leave,
and grow old wanting to get back to.
John Ed Pearce

FRIENDSHIP

Friendship is born at that moment when one person says to
another: "What! You too? I thought I was the only one.
C.S. Lewis

Don't walk behind me; I may not lead. Don't walk in front of me; I
may not follow. Just walk beside me and be my friend.
Albert Camus

A friend is one who believes in you when you
have ceased to believe in yourself.
Unknown

You can make more friends in two months by becoming
interested in other people than you can in two years trying
to get people interested in you.
Dale Carnegie

A best friend is like a four leave clover,
hard to find and lucky to have.
Unknown

A negative friend is worse than an enemy.
Unknown

A friend is like an eagle, you don't find them flying in flocks.
Unknown

A friend is one that knows you as you are, understands
where you have been, accepts what you have become,
and still, gently allows you to grow.
William Shakespeare

A day spent with friends, is a day well spent.
Unknown

GOALS

The future belongs to those who believe
in the beauty of their dreams.
Eleanor Roosevelt

Everything starts as somebody's daydream.
Larry Niven

People with goals succeed because they know where they are going.
Earl Nightingale

Happiness, wealth, and success are the by products of goal setting;
they cannot be the goals themselves.
Denis Waitley

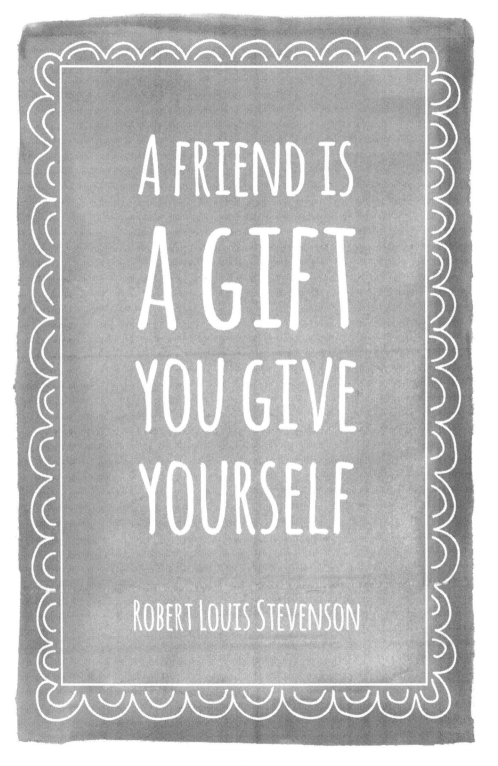

A FRIEND IS A GIFT YOU GIVE YOURSELF

ROBERT LOUIS STEVENSON

It is never too late to be what you might have been.
George Eliot

It's the possibility of having a dream come true
that makes life interesting.
Paulo Coelho

Obstacles are those frightful things you see
when you take your eyes off your goals.
Henry Ford

We come this way but once. We can either tiptoe through life
and hope we get to death without being badly bruised
or we can live a full, complete life achieving our goals and
realizing our wildest dreams.
Bob Proctor

Winners must have two things: definite goals
and a burning desire to achieve them.
Unknown

No matter how many goals you have achieved,
you must set your sights on a higher one.
Jessica Savitch

Success is the progressive realization of predetermined,
worthwhile, personal goals.
Paul J. Meyer

When it is obvious that the goals cannot be reached,
don't adjust the goals, adjust the action steps.
Confucius

Discipline is the bridge between goals and accomplishment.
Jim Rohn

Do more than is required. What is the distance between someone
who achieves their goals consistently and those who spend their
lives and careers merely following? The extra mile.
Gary Ryan Blair

Think little goals and expect little achievements.
Think big goals and win big success.
David Joseph Schwartz

Learn from the past, set vivid, detailed goals for the future, and live
in the only moment of time over which you have any control: now.
Denis Waitley

One way to keep momentum going is to have
constantly greater goals.
Michael Korda

You need to overcome the tug of people against you
as you reach for high goals.
George S. Patton

Setting goals is the first step in turning the invisible into the visible.
Tony Robbins

You have to find out what's right for you, so it's trial and error. You
are going to be all right if you accept realistic goals for yourself.
Teri Garr

Set your goals high, and don't stop till you get there.
Bo Jackson

My personal goals are to be happy,
healthy and to be surrounded by loved ones.
Kiana Tom

No matter how carefully you plan your goals they will never be
more than pipe dreams unless you pursue them with gusto.
W. Clement Stone

What keeps me going is goals.
Muhammad Ali

If you are not making the progress that you would like to make and are capable of making, it is simply because your goals are not clearly defined.
Paul J. Meyer

Goals are not only absolutely necessary to motivate us. They are essential to really keep us alive.
Robert H. Schuller

If you go to work on your goals, your goals will go to work on you. If you go to work on your plan, your plan will go to work on you. Whatever good things we build end up building us.
Jim Rohn

Goals must never be from your ego, but problems that cry for a solution.
Robert H. Schuller

You're forced to think about what your goals are and you clarify them because you're taking this journey with another person and you need to be open with your partner.
Sarah Michelle Gellar

Your goals, minus your doubts, equal your reality.
Ralph Marston

If you don't accept failure as a possibility, you don't set high goals, you don't branch out, you don't try - you don't take the risk.
Rosalynn Carter

GRATITUDE

Happiness doesn't depend on what we have, but it does depend on how we feel toward what we have. We can be happy with little and miserable with much.
William Dempster Hoard

How lucky I am to have something that makes
saying goodbye so hard.
A.A. Milne

It is only with gratitude that life becomes rich.
Dietrich Bonhoeffer

Whatever you appreciate and give thanks for
will increase in your life.
Sanaya Roman

Give thanks for a little and you will find a lot.
The Hausa of Nigeria

If all misfortunes were laid in one common heap whence everyone
must take an equal portion, most people would be contented to take
their own and depart.
Socrates

We tend to forget that happiness doesn't come as a result of
getting something we don't have, but rather of recognizing
and appreciating what we do have.
Frederick Keonig

Whatever we think about & thank about, we bring about.
Dr John F Demartini

When I started counting my blessings, my whole life turned around.
Willie Nelson

Be thankful for what you have; you'll end up having more.
If you concentrate on what you don't have, you will never,
ever have enough.
Oprah Winfrey

If the only prayer you said in your whole life was 'thank you',
that would suffice.
Meister Eckhart

Let us rise up and be thankful, for if we didn't learn a lot today,
at least we learned a little, and if we didn't learn a little,
at least we didn't get sick, and if we got sick,
at least we didn't die; so, let us be thankful.
Buddha

No duty is more urgent than that of returning thanks.
Unknown

Let us be grateful to people who make us happy; they are the
charming gardeners who make our souls blossom.
Marcel Proust

He is a wise man who does not grieve for the things which
he has not, but rejoices for those which he has.
Epictetus

We can only be said to be alive in those moments when
our hearts are conscious of our treasures.
Thornton Wilder

Gratitude can transform common days into thanksgivings,
turn routine jobs into joy, and change ordinary
opportunities into blessings.
William Arthur Ward

We often take for granted the very things that most
deserve our gratitude.
Cynthia Ozick

There are only two ways to live your life. One is as though nothing
is a miracle. The other is as though everything is a miracle.
Albert Einstein

Gratitude is a vaccine, an antitoxin, and an antiseptic.
John Henry Jowett

Gratitude is riches. Complaint is poverty.
Doris Day

What if you gave someone a gift, and they neglected to thank you for it-would you be likely to give them another? Life is the same way. In order to attract more of the blessings that life has to offer, you must truly appreciate what you already have.
Ralph Marston

Gratefulness is the key to a happy life that we hold in our hands, because if we are not grateful, then no matter how much we have we will not be happy — because we will always want to have something else or something more.
Brother David Steindl-Rast

If you concentrate on finding whatever is good in every situation, you will discover that your life will suddenly be filled with gratitude, a feeling that nurtures the soul.
Rabbi Harold Kushner

Be thankful that you don't already have everything you desire,
If you did, what would there be to look forward to?
Be thankful when you don't know something,
For it gives you the opportunity to learn.
Be thankful for the difficult times.
During those times you grow.
Be thankful for your limitations,
Because they give you opportunities for improvement.
Be thankful for each new challenge,
Because it will build your strength and character.
Be thankful for your mistakes,
They will teach you valuable lessons.
Be thankful when you're tired and weary,
Because it means you've made a difference.
It is easy to be thankful for the good things.
A life of rich fulfillment comes to those who are
also thankful for the setbacks.
GRATITUDE can turn a negative into a positive.
Find a way to be thankful for your troubles
and they can become your blessings.
Unknown

HAPPINESS IS NOT BY CHANCE BUT BY CHOICE

Jim Rohn

HAPPINESS

Happiness is the highest level of success.
Unknown

Action may not bring happiness,
but there is no happiness without action.
William James

Happiness is not getting what you want,
but wanting what you've got.
Unknown

Think of all the beauty still left around you and be happy.
Anne Frank

A truly happy person is one who can enjoy
the scenery while on a detour.
Unknown

Happiness depends upon ourselves.
Aristotle

The foolish man seeks happiness in the distance,
the wise grows it under his feet.
James Oppenheim

Now and then it's good to pause in our pursuit of happiness
and just be happy.
Guillaume Apollinaire

To be happy for an hour, get drunk; to be happy for a year,
fall in love; to be happy for life, take up gardening.
Chinese Proverb

When I eat with my friends, it is a moment of real pleasure,
when I really enjoy my life.
Monica Bellucci

No matter what has happened,
you too have the power to enjoy yourself.
Allen Klein

The moments of happiness we enjoy take us by surprise.
It is not that we seize them, but that they seize us.
Ashley Montagu

Happiness cannot be traveled to, owned, earned, worn or consumed.
Happiness is the spiritual experience of living every minute with
love, grace and gratitude.
Denis Waitley

Happiness often sneaks in through a door you
didn't know you left open.
John Barrymore

Happiness is where we find it, but rarely where we seek it.
J Petit Senn

Happiness held is the seed; happiness shared is the flower.
Unknown

HEALTH

The greatest wealth is health.
Virgil

Whenever I feel the need to exercise, I lie down until it goes away.
Paul Terry

Use your health, even to the point of wearing it out. That is what it
is for. Spend all you have before you die; do not outlive yourself.
George Bernard Shaw

A man too busy to take care of his health is like a mechanic
too busy to take care of his tools.
Spanish Proverb

A vigorous five-mile walk will do more good for an unhappy
but otherwise healthy adult than all the medicine and
psychology in the world.
Paul Dudley White

The reason I exercise is for the quality of life I enjoy.
Kenneth H. Cooper

I think it's more important to be fit so that you can be healthy
and enjoy activities than it is to have a good body.
Rachel Blanchard

Some people like going to the pub; I enjoy going to the gym.
Frank Bruno

A man's health can be judged by which he takes two at a time
– pills or stairs.
Joan Welsh

Cheerfulness, sir, is the principle ingredient
in the composition of health.
Arthur Murphy

Eat well, drink in moderation, and sleep sound,
in these three good health abound.
Proverb

INSPIRATIONAL

The past is over...forget it. The future holds hope...reach for it.
Charles R. Swindoll

If you can dream it, you can do it.
Walt Disney

Those who don't believe in magic will never find it.
Roald Dahl

Faith is taking the first step even when you can't see the whole staircase.
Martin Luther King Jr.

Isn't it nice to think that tomorrow is a new day with no mistakes in it yet?
L.M. Montgomery

What's meant to be will always find a way.
Trisha Yearwood

Be yourself; everyone else is already taken.
Oscar Wilde

Here's to the crazy ones. The misfits. The rebels. The troublemakers. The round pegs in the square holes. The ones who see things differently. They're not fond of rules. And they have no respect for the status quo. You can quote them, disagree with them, glorify or vilify them. About the only thing you can't do is ignore them. Because they change things. They push the human race forward. And while some may see them as the crazy ones, we see genius. Because the people who are crazy enough to think they can change the world, are the ones who do.
Apple Inc.

To live is the rarest thing in the world. Most people exist, that is all.
Oscar Wilde

No dreamer is ever too small; no dream is ever too big.
Unknown

Some people say you are going the wrong way, when it is simply a way of your own.
Angelina Jolie

Though no one can go back and make a brand new start, anyone can start from now and make a brand new ending.
Carl Bard

In the midst of winter, I found there was,
within me an invincible summer.
Albert Camus

Make each day your masterpiece.
John Wooden

Destiny is not a matter of chance, it is a matter of choice.
William Jennings

Hope is like a road in the country; there was never a road, but when
many people walk on it, the road comes into existence.
Lyn Yutang

The journey is the reward.
Chinese Proverb

Don't count the days, make the days count.
Muhammad Ali

The steeper the mountain the harder the climb,
the better the view from the finishing line.
Unknown

Have a heart that never hardens, a temper that never tires,
a touch that never hurts.
Charles Dickens

Life is not about waiting for the storm to pass.
It's about learning to dance in the rain.
Unknown

Your worth consists in what you are and not in what you have.
Thomas Edison

My philosophy is that not only are you responsible
for your life, but doing the best at this moment
puts you in the best place for the next moment.
Oprah Winfrey

KINDNESS

Never believe that a few caring people can't change the world
For, indeed, that's all who ever have.
Margaret Mead

Wherever there is a human being
there is an opportunity for kindness.
Seneca

Everything we do affects other people.
Luke Ford

If you can't say anything nice, don't say anything at all.
Thumper's Mother, Bambi

If you judge people, you have no time to love them.
Mother Teresa

Be kind, for everyone you meet is fighting a harder battle.
Plato

The best portion of a good man's life – his little, nameless,
unremembered acts of kindness.
William Wordsworth

Kind words can be short and easy to speak,
but their echoes are truly endless.
Mother Teresa

LIFE LESSONS

Sometimes life gives us lessons sent in ridiculous packaging.
Dar Williams

In the race for quality, there is no finish line.
David T. Kearns

That which doesn't kill us makes us stronger.
Friedrich Nietzche

NO ONE CAN MAKE YOU FEEL INFERIOR WITHOUT YOUR CONSENT

Eleanor Roosevelt

If you don't stand for something you will fall for anything.
Malcolm X

Never laugh at live dragons.
J.R.R. Tolkien

It is better to be hated for what you are
than to be loved for what you are not.
André Gide

Always laugh when you can, it is cheap medicine.
Lord Byron

Giving up doesn't always mean you are weak.
Sometimes it means that you are strong enough to let go.
Unknown

Our life is frittered away by detail. Simplify, simplify.
Henry David Thoreau

He who has a why to live can bear almost any how.
Friedrich Nietzsche

The Four Agreements
1.Be impeccable with your word.
2.Don't take anything personally.
3.Don't make assumptions.
4.Always do your best.
Don Miguel Ruiz

We laugh to survive.
Mary Anne Radmacher

A tough lesson in life that one has to learn is that
not everybody wishes you well.
Dan Rather

The greatest lesson in life is to know that even
fools are right sometimes.
Horace

In school, you're taught a lesson and then given a test.
In life, you're given a test that teaches you a lesson.
Tom Bodett

Women and cats will do as they please, and men and dogs
should relax and get used to the idea.
Robert A. Heinlein

Take time to play!
Ask for what you want.
Laugh.
Live loudly.
Be avid.
Learn a new thing.
Be Yourself!
Mary Anne Radmacher

Life is really simple, but we insist on making it complicated.
Confucius

Feeling sorry for yourself, and your present condition, is not only a
waste of energy but the worst habit you could possibly have.
Dale Carnegie

It's never too late - never too late to start over,
never too late to be happy.
Jane Fonda

Life is too important to be taken seriously.
Oscar Wilde

Believe and act as if it was impossible to fail.
Charles Kettering

You can't do anything about the length of your life,
but you can do something about its width and depth.
Evan Esar

Don't approach a goat from the front, a horse from the back,
or a fool from any side.
Yiddish Proverb

If you want to be happy, be.
Leo Tolstoy

Work hard and be nice to people.
Unknown

If we treated everyone we meet with the same affection we bestow
upon our favorite cat, they, too, would purr.
Martin Delany

Be a light, a lifeboat or a ladder.
Unknown

If you want something you've never had,
you have to do something you've never done.
Unknown

Only look down on someone when you are helping them up.
Unknown

Hatred is a boomerang which is sure to hit you
harder than the one at whom you throw it.
Unknown

People grow through experience if they meet life honestly and
courageously. This is how character is built.
Eleanor Roosevelt

LOVE

The first duty of love is to listen.
Unknown

Love is like a virus. It can happen to anybody at any time.
Maya Angelou

I'm selfish, impatient and a little insecure. I make mistakes, I am out of control and at times hard to handle. But if you can't handle me at my worst, then you sure as hell don't deserve me at my best.
Marilyn Monroe

When God created Man she was only kidding.
Unknown

Love is the irresistible desire to be irresistibly desired.
Mark Twain

It is not a lack of love,
but a lack of friendship that makes unhappy marriages.
Friedrich Nietzsche

Love doesn't make the world go round;
love is what makes the ride worthwhile.
Elizabeth Browning

Love is friendship, set on fire.
Jeremy Taylor

Love is composed of a single soul inhabiting two bodies.
Aristotle

You may only be someone in the world,
but to someone else, you may be the world.
Unknown

MISTAKES

The greatest mistake you can make in life is to be continually fearing you will make one.
Elbert Hubbard

When written in Chinese, the word "crisis" is composed of two characters. One represents danger and the other represents opportunity.
John F. Kennedy

Life can only be understood backwards,
but it must be lived forwards.
Kierkegaard

Mistakes are always forgivable,
if one has the courage to admit them.
Bruce Lee

Failure is simply the opportunity to begin again,
this time more intelligently.
Henry Ford

I have tried 99 times and have failed,
but on the 100th time came success.
Albert Einstein

A life spent making mistakes is not only more
honorable but more useful a life spent doing nothing.
George Bernard Shaw

Failures are the finger posts on the road to achievement.
C S Lewis

If we will be quiet and ready enough,
we shall find compensation in every disappointment.
Henry David Thoreau

Fall seven times, stand up eight.
Japanese Proverb

Try and fail, but don't fail to try.
Stephen Kraggwa

MONEY

A bank is a place where they lend you an umbrella in fair weather
and ask for it back when it begins to rain.
Robert Frost

Money won't create success. The freedom to make it will.
Nelson Mandela

Don't go around saying the world owes you a living.
The world owes you nothing. It was here first.
Mark Twain

Money itself won't bring happiness,
but it sure makes paying the bills easier.
Thomas J. Vilord

There are plenty of ways to get ahead. The first is so basic I'm
almost embarrassed to say it; spend less than you earn.
Paul Clitheroe

Borrowed money shortens time.
Chinese Proverb

Don't judge each day by the harvest you reap,
but by the seeds that you plant.
Robert Louis Stevenson

Cannot people realize how large of an income is thrift?
Cicero

Better bread with water than cake with trouble.
Russian proverb

I'm living so far beyond my income that we may
almost be said to be living apart.
E E Cummings

MOTIVATIONAL

Twenty years from now you will be more disappointed by the things
you didn't do than by the ones you did do. So throw off the bowlines.
Sail away from the safe harbor. Catch the trade winds in your sails.
Explore. Dream. Discover.
Mark Twain

Done is better than perfect.
Unknown

A good idea today, is better than a perfect idea tomorrow.
Unknown

When you think you can't... revisit a previous triumph.
Jack Canfield

Great works are performed not by strength, but perseverance.
Dr. Samuel Johnson

When everything feels like an uphill struggle,
just think of the view from the top.
Unknown

The best way out is always through.
Robert Frost

You cannot plough a field by turning it over in your mind.
Unknown

Don't limit your challenges; challenge your limits.
Unknown

The greatest happiness is to transform your feelings in action.
Madame de Stael

Triumph is just a little "umph" added to try.
Unknown

You cannot find peace by avoiding life.
Virginia Woolf

If you are going through hell, keep going.
Winston S. Churchill

Adversity has the effect of eliciting talents which,
in prosperous circumstances would have lain dormant.
Horace

The journey of a thousand miles must begin with a SINGLE STEP

Lao Tzu

To climb steep hills requires a slow pace at first.
William Shakespeare

And in the end it's not the years in your life that count.
It's the life in your years.
Abraham Lincoln

NATURE

Look deep into nature,
and then you will understand everything better.
Albert Einstein

Cats have it all – admiration, an endless sleep,
and company only when they want it.
Rod Mckuen

A black cat crossing your path signifies that the
animal is going somewhere.
Groucho Marx

There is a way that nature speaks, that land speaks. Most of the
time we are simply not patient enough, quiet enough, to pay
attention to the story.
Linda Hogan

Accuse not Nature, she hath done her part; Do thou but thine.
John Milton

Flowers are the earth laughing.
Ralph Waldo Emerson

A pent up cat becomes a lion.
Proverb

My hamster died yesterday. Fell asleep at the wheel.
Frank Carson

Even the woodpecker owes his success to the fact that he uses his head and keeps pecking away until he finishes the job he started.
Coleman Cox

I like pigs. Dogs look up at us. Cats look down on us.
Pigs treat us like equals.
Winston Churchill

I don't kill flies. I like to mess with their minds. I hold them above globes. They freak out and yell, 'Whoa, I'm way too high.'
Jim Koser

A racehorse is the only animal that can take thousands of people for a ride at the same time.
Herbert Prochnow

A dog is the only thing on earth that loves you more than he loves himself.
Josh Billings

Bad weather always looks worse through a window.
John Kieran

Dogs come when they're called; cats take a message and get back to you later.
Mary Bly

I find that duck's opinion of me is greatly influenced by whether or not I have bread.
Mitch Hedberg

I have a dog that's half pit bull, half poodle.
Not so much of a guard dog, but a vicious gossip.
Billiam Coronel

POSITIVE THINKING

Attitude is everything.
Charles Swindoll

The happiness of your life depends on the quality of your thoughts.
Unknown

All that we are, is a result of what we have thought.
Buddha

The greatest discovery of all time is that a person can change his future by merely changing his attitude.
Oprah Winfrey

Whether you think you can or think you can't, you're right.
Henry Ford

We cannot always control what goes on outside,
but we can control what goes on inside.
Unknown

A pessimist sees the difficulty in every opportunity; an optimist sees the opportunity in every difficulty.
Winston S. Churchill

If you can imagine it, you can achieve it.
If you can dream it, you can become it.
William Arthur Ward

Whatever you can do or dream you can, begin it.
Boldness has genius, power and magic in it!
Johann Wolfgang Von Goethe

To accomplish great things we must not only act, but also dream;
not only plan, but also believe.
Anatole France

Yesterday is but today's memory, and tomorrow is today's dream.
Khalil Gibran

SCIENCE

The process of scientific discovery is, in effect,
a continual flight from wonder.
Albert Einstein

The possession of knowledge does not kill the sense of wonder and
mystery. There is always more mystery.
Anais Nin

The time-travel convention will be held two weeks ago.
Unknown

Science may set limits to knowledge,
but should not set limits to imagination.
Bertrand Russell

New discoveries in science will continue to create a thousand new
frontiers for those who still would adventure.
Herbert Hoover

I am among those who think that science has great beauty.
A scientist in his laboratory is not only a technician:
he is also a child placed before natural phenomena which
impress him like a fairy tale.
Marie Curie

SUCCESS

Never let the fear of striking out get in your way.
Babe Ruth

Do or do not, there is no try.
Jedi Master Yoda, Star Wars

Winners never quit and quitters never win.
Vince Lombardi

You can't win unless you learn how to lose.
Kareem Abdul-Jabbar

To be a champion,
you have to believe in yourself when nobody else will.
Sugar Ray Robinson

If you do things well, do them better.
Be daring, be first, be different, be just.
Anita Roddick

A business absolutely devoted to service will have only one worry
about profits. They will be embarrassingly large.
Henry Ford

Never burn bridges. Today's junior jerk, tomorrow's senior partner.
Sigourney Weaver

A real entrepreneur is somebody who has
no safety net underneath them.
Henry Kravis

Drive your business. Let not your business drive you.
Benjamin Franklin

Success is walking from failure to failure
with no loss of enthusiasm.
Winston Churchill

The greatest barrier to success is the fear of failure.
Sven Goran Eriksson

We are what we repeatedly do.
Excellence then is not an act but a habit.
Aristotle

Eighty percent of success is showing up.
Woody Allen

Failure is simply the opportunity to begin again, this time more
intelligently.
Henry Ford

I don't know the key to success, but the key to failure is trying to please everybody.
Bill Cosby

Early to bed and early to rise makes a man healthy, wealthy and wise.
Benjamin Franklin

People become successful the minute they decide to.
Harvey Mackay

Good things come to those who hustle while they wait.
Unknown

Approach the start of each day with something in mind and end the day with one word...DONE.
Unknown

Success is not the key to happiness. Happiness is the key to success. If you love what you are doing, you will be successful.
Herman Cain

One sound idea is all you need to achieve success.
Napoleon Hill

Whatever you are, be a good one.
Abraham Lincoln

There is only one thing that makes a dream impossible to achieve: the fear of failure.
Paulo Coelho

To be yourself in a world that is constantly trying to make you something else is the greatest accomplishment.
Ralph Waldo Emerson

People who enjoy meetings should not be in charge of anything.
Thomas Sowell

WORRY

You wouldn't worry so much about what others think of
you if you realized how seldom they do.
Eleanor Roosevelt

Worry often gives a small thing a big shadow.
Swedish proverb

If you can't sleep, then get up and do something instead
of lying there and worrying.
It's the worry that gets you,
not the loss of sleep.
Dale Carnegie

It ain't no use putting up your umbrella till it rains.
Alice Caldwell Rice

Hurrying and worrying are not the same as strength.
Nigerian Proverb

Perpetual worry will get you to one place ahead of time
- the cemetery.
Unknown

A man 99 years old was asked to what he attributed his longevity. I
reckon, he said, with a twinkle in his eye, it's because most nights I
went to bed and slept when I should have sat up and worried.
Garson Kanin

Why Worry?
An Irish philosophy

There are only two things to worry about,
Either you are well or you are sick.

If you are well,
Then there is nothing to worry about.

But if you are sick,
There are only two things to worry about.
Either you will get well or you die.

If you get well,
There is nothing to worry about.

If you die,
There are only two things to worry about.
Either you will go to heaven or hell.

If you go to heaven there is nothing to worry about.

But if you go to hell,
You'll be so damn busy shaking hands with friends you
won't have time to worry!

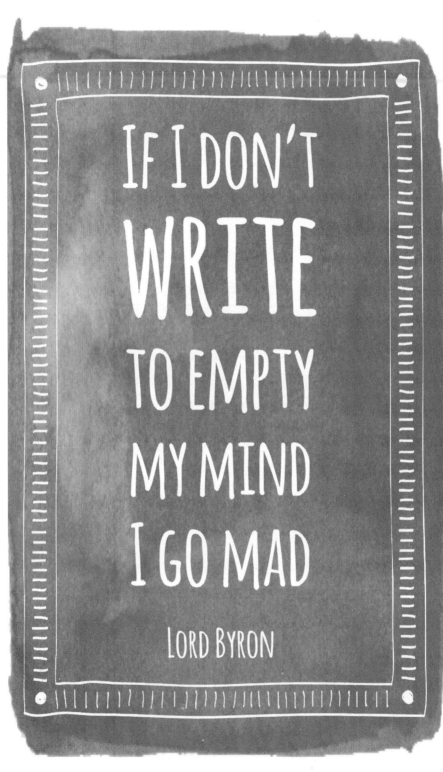

IF I DON'T **WRITE** TO EMPTY MY MIND I GO MAD

Lord Byron

WRITING

I am a writer who came of a sheltered life. A sheltered life can
be a daring life as well. For all serious daring starts from within.
Eudora Welty

If there's a book that you want to read,
but it hasn't been written yet, then you must write it.
Toni Morrison

When you are describing,
A shape, or sound, or tint;
Don't state the matter plainly,
But put it in a hint;
And learn to look at all things,
With a sort of mental squint.
Lewis Carroll

When I write, I enjoy myself so much that what is
being written really needs no reader.
Guillermo Cabrera Infante

You write your first draft with your heart and you re-write with
your head. The first key to writing is to write, not to think.
Sean Connery

A book comes and says, 'Write me.' My job is to try to serve it to the
best of my ability, which is never good enough, but all I can do is
listen to it, do what it tells me and collaborate.
Madeleine L'engle

A mediocre mind thinks it writes divinely;
a good mind thinks it writes reasonably.
Jean De La Bruyere

A notebook can be a clearing in the forest of your life, a place where
you can be alone and content as you play with outrage and wonder,
details and gossip, language and dreams, plots and subplots,
perceptions and small epiphanies.
Ralph Flether

Any fool can write a novel but it takes a real genius to sell it.
J G Ballard

Don't get it right, just get it written.
James Thurber

Easy reading is damned hard writing.
Nathaniel Hawthorne

Every piece of writing... starts from what I call a grit... a sight or sound, a sentence or happening that does not pass away... but quite inexplicably lodges in the mind.
Rumer Godden

Every writer I know has trouble writing.
Joseph Heller

He writes so well he makes me feel like putting the quill back in the goose.
Fred Allen

I don't care who you are. When you sit down to write the first page of your screenplay, in your head you're also writing your Oscar acceptance speech.
Nora Ephron

I don't like to write, but I love to have written.
Michael Kanin

I just sit at a typewriter and curse a bit.
P G Wodehouse

I lived to write, and wrote to live.
Samuel Rogers

I love writing but hate starting. The page is awfully white and it says, 'You may have fooled some of the people some of the time but those days are over, giftless. I'm not your agent and I'm not your mommy. I'm a white piece of paper, you wanna dance with me? And I really, really don't.
Aaron Sorkin

I put all my genius into my life; I put only my talent into my works.
Oscar Wilde

I write when I'm inspired, and I see to it that I'm inspired at nine
O'clock every morning.
Peter De Vries

I don't suffer from writers block, I can suffer from
'getting to the desk to write' block.
Jackie Collins

Authors like cats because they are such quiet, lovable, wise
creatures, and cats like authors for the same reasons.
Robertson Davies

HELLO

I'm Rossi, I can often be found upside down on my yellow yoga mat, journal writing and getting creatively messy. I am a quote addict, a gadget geek and an aspiring minimalist. I also consider myself to be a cake magnet, as I can't walk past a cake without being attracted to it. You too?

Once a reluctant journal writer myself (I was scared of the blank page) I discovered the benefits of keeping a journal while studying Psychology and Visual Communications.

Some of my favorite things are sleeping, reading with my legs up the wall, opening parcels, pop-up books, action movies, the smell of blown out candles, iPhoneography and being a tourist. I am allergic to mathematics and I look like I am taking part in a flash mob dance for one whenever a wasp comes near me.

Can I take this opportunity to say a massive THANK YOU for reading my first book and I really hope it has helped you in some way. Hopefully your journals should be a million miles away from tho soary blank notebooks they once were.

For any questions, suggestions or thoughts please feel free to contact me at hello@rossifox.com.

Thanks a million and all the best,
Rossi

MAY GOOD LUCK
BE YOUR FRIEND IN
WHATEVER YOU DO
AND MAY TROUBLE
ALWAYS BE A
STRANGER TO YOU

Irish Blessing

Notes / Doodles / Plans For World Domination

Made in the USA
Middletown, DE
18 December 2016